A CHOICE OF POPE'S VERSE

A Choice of
POPE'S VERSE

Selected and with an Introduction
by

PETER PORTER

FABER AND FABER
3 Queen Square
London

First published in 1971
by Faber and Faber Limited
3 Queen Square London WC1
Printed in Great Britain by
The Bowering Press Plymouth
All rights reserved

ISBN 0 571 09292 6
(Faber Paper Covered Edition)

ISBN 0 571 09291 8
(Hard Bound Edition)

Introduction © Peter Porter, 1971
This selection © Faber & Faber, 1971

The editor and publishers wish to thank Methuen & Co. Ltd. for permission to use the text of the Twickenham edition of *The Poems of Alexander Pope*, edited by John Butt.

Contents

Introduction	*page*	9
Summer. The Second Pastoral, or Alexis		41
An Essay on Criticism		44
The Temple of Fame		59
Windsor Forest		62
The Rape of the Lock (Cantos III-V)		66
A Farewell to London. In the Year 1715		81
Ode on Solitude		83
Verses Occasion'd by an Etc. at the End of Mr. D'Urfy's Name in the Title to one of his Plays		84
To Mr. John Moore, Author of the Celebrated Worm-Powder		87
Three Epitaphs on John Hewet and Sarah Drew		89
The Lamentation of Grumdalclitch, for the Loss of Grildrig. A Pastoral		90
The Words of the King of Brobdingnag, as he held Captain Gulliver between his Finger and Thumb for the Inspection of the Sages and Learned Men of the Court		93
An Essay on Man. The Second Epistle		94
Moral Essays. Epistle II. To a Lady. Of the Characters of Women		103
Epistle III. To Allen Lord Bathurst		112
An Epistle from Mr. Pope, to Dr. Arbuthnot		119
The First Epistle of the Second Book of Horace Imitated. To Augustus		132
The Second Epistle of the Second Book of Horace Imitated		137

The Seventh Epistle of the First Book of Horace
    Imitated in the Manner of Dr. Swift   *page* 138
The Fourth Satire of Dr. John Donne, Dean of St.
    Paul's, Versifyed   141
The Dunciad. Version of 1742   142
Imitations of English Poets: Earl of Dorset   150
On Silence   152
Epigrams, Etc.   154
Index of first lines and extracts   157

8

Introduction

Pope's reputation is unassailable. Only Chaucer, Milton and Donne are considered his equals and Shakespeare alone his superior. But this does not mean that he is much read outside universities. The temper of our age and the mixture of excitement and suspicion in its reading habits makes Pope an unpopular poet. The modern poetic renaissance turns out to be the phenomenon of more people reading fewer poems. The Modernist anti-canon is narrower than the old Academic one. A young public (those who read or write poetry under thirty) will not spare time from reading Blake to enjoy Pope. Perhaps their suspicion of him is sharpened by the feeling that he belongs to the scholars and that one has to have a good deal of knowledge oneself to enjoy him. Certainly, few poets are so much commented on academically and he has inspired a great deal of superb scholarship, much of it recently. Has any English poet benefited from such magnificent editing as Pope received in the complete Twickenham edition? Without the erudition and patience of the men who compiled it, the general reader would be lost among the complexities of variant readings. So the excuse for making yet another selection of his poetry must be the desire to introduce him to an audience which is put off by false impressions of his work. Nobody who has been to school at all can be wholly ignorant of Pope's famous poems, but the chances are that what he read then he didn't like and that ever since prevailing fashions have reinforced his hostility. The person who thinks that poetry began with Ezra Pound, was reborn with Ginsberg and now lives in San Francisco, may still be able to get signals from the past—from Blake, from Whitman, sometimes from Shakespeare and even, unaccountably, from Wordsworth. But he'll be jammed against receiving Pope.

9

Even some Anti-Modernist figures must share the blame for this; Robert Graves for one. In *The Crowning Privilege*, Graves dismissed Pope with the observation that English poets wore their own hair. Graves has a fine head of hair but it's less distinguished than Pope's wig. The more expected difficulty comes from two aspects of the same thing—Augustan artificiality and the heroic couplet. It's true that no great poet besides Pope has ever put so many eggs in one basket (though think of Domenico Scarlatti in music, with his five hundred and fifty sonatas in binary form). Blank verse as practised by the Jacobeans or rhyming stanzas by the Romantics are neither as restricted nor as monotonous as the regular iambic pentameter couplet. The reason is not hard to find: the exigencies of rhyming dictate the sentence construction. But Pope's genius shines more strongly in these limits. Ninety per cent of his verse is in heroic couplets, yet there is more variety, rhythmical subtlety and relief from mechanical formulae in Pope than in any English poet after Shakespeare. He can be utterly limpid but he can also be grotesque and extreme. He is master of the created world—aware of every part of the classical inheritance, but with so much nature as well. His way with the surface of the world of his own time is so authoritative, he cannot be called the slave of Greece and Rome. Besides, the couplet is quite unclassical—it has no links with Homer and Virgil. It's easily forgotten that the Augustans were the heirs of the Restoration writers, who valued realism as much as they did wit. Compare, for instance, Restoration plays with Molière—the English not only show a much greater complication but they are more deeply rooted in contemporary life and they write in prose. It was the special task of Pope's genius to do in poetry what Wycherley and Congreve did in the theatre. He had to illuminate the *prosaic* imagination of the Restoration, to tool up poetry to deal with the new literalness, represented by the almost 'touchable' quality of dialogue in Vanbrugh's plays. To continue the manufacturing metaphor—poetry is the most durable material in literature. Pope rediscovered how to work it for a modern market whose real interest was in social comedy and not in tragedy. Dryden had been there before him, but Dryden was a party man, a polemicist working to a thesis. Pope, the born Catholic, had none of Dryden's interest in religious controversy and little of his passionate involvement in day-to-day politics. Pope seems, on the other hand, to have been born with an innate knowledge of how the world works. He had that extraordinary faculty of understanding things without having experienced them. His material needs were all in books and from his earliest years he absorbed the literature and philosophy of the past. Not just the classics but the speculative and scientific authors of the seventeenth century. He added to this knowledge throughout his life, of course, but his first poems are as finished if not as ambitious as his later masterpieces. *The Essay on Criticism* is as complete a critique of humanity as *The Essay on Man*, and the cast of his mind led him to the more exegetical subject when he was young and the looser, more humanistic one in middle age.

For an artist of Pope's kind (and the combination of precocity with good judgment is rare), the divine commandment was simply to create. His sense of form was so great that the spiritual crises of his life had little influence on his literary productions. No doubt Pope's life story ('this long Disease, My Life') is worth some psychoanalytical study and it's improbable that he was happy. But the bulwarks between the sick man and the healthy artist were so strong, no insecurity in the one could disturb the other. And his age supported him—

not just with patronage and friendship, but by its climate of opinion and the expectation it had of its authors. Grub Street pursued him with calumnies, and translation took up much of his time, but by the end of his life he had produced a dozen major poems, each a masterpiece. The fact that his two longest poems are parody-epics is pure gain. He was never tempted to emulate Homer and Virgil on their own ground and devote his life's work to an abortion like *Paradise Lost* (the term is not meant to be rude: it seems a just description of Milton's attempt to construct a native English epic. I am not impressed by the argument that the Christian concept of the Fall needed its epic to match the pagan ones. Pope seems not to have been either, for he always avoided the grandiose just as he did the facetious. His own comment on Milton was—

> Milton's strong pinion now not Heav'n can bound,
> Now serpent-like in prose he sweeps the ground,
> In quibbles, Angel and Archangel join,
> And God the Father turns a School-Divine).

Instead, Pope pioneered the medium-length social poem which is to Miltonic what comic-opera is to *opera seria*. In it he wrote four flawless poems, *The Essay on Criticism*, *The Rape of the Lock*, *An Epistle to a Lady* and *The Epistle to Dr. Arbuthnot*. Most of the remainder of his major works are almost as good. And the great triumphs of English verse since his day have been on the scale and along the social lines which Pope laid down.

Pope's Lyricism

If anyone finds the following passage unlyrical, then he's in an important stylistic quandary. It's from *An Epistle to a Lady*, the Second of the *Moral Essays*.

Narcissa's nature, tolerably mild,
To make a wash, would hardly stew a child,
Has ev'n been prov'd to grant a Lover's pray'r,
And paid a Tradesman once to make him stare,
Gave alms at Easter, in a Christmas trim,
And made a Widow happy, for a whim.
Why then declare Good-nature is her scorn,
When 'tis by that alone she can be born?
Why pique all mortals, yet affect a name?
A fool to Pleasure, and a slave to Fame:
Now deep in Taylor and the Book of Martyrs,
Now drinking citron with his Grace and Chartres.
Now Conscience chills her, and now Passion burns;
And Atheism and Religion take their turns;
A very Heathen in the carnal part,
Yet still a sad, good Christian at her heart.

When prose took over the toothsome bits from verse (facts, stories, who's sleeping with whom, etc.), poetry was left only the lyrical and the aphoristic. The Romantics capitalized on this, and we don't, as a rule, read the lengthy poems they wrote in the older tradition: instead we esteem only their lyrics. This is perfectly natural, provided we don't believe that only one sort of lyricism is desirable. Like tunes in music, lyricism is what people go for in poetry, but two centuries of refining it have given us unadventurous palates. *The Golden Treasury* isn't the only culprit: we tend to sift all our poetry for the lyrical passages. In this sense Pope is an antediluvian poet—it is the total impact of his work which is lyrical, not the arrangement of individual passages, the cunning mimesis or the Sitwellian procession of sounds. What he means actually counts, and a passage such as the one quoted above has more ways of pleasing than by its mellifluousness. It is as beautifully prepared as *The Lotos Eaters* and as well-judged as sound. But there is no escapist element, no smell of poetry about it. The syntax is conversational, yet highly artificial, having been arranged to provide antithesis and avoid clumsy line breaks. The whole construction is economical and the iambic rhythm is musical in the correct sense. (Literary critics should learn that musical is not a synonym of lyrical—a 12/8 harpsichord gigue where the page is black with notes is just as musical as an oboe cantabile.) Pope is also joking and is not above using plain sarcasm. There are limits, he observes, to the lady's self-love. There are things she won't do and even some she will, such as pleasing a lover (once). Her counterpart today is still fobbing off tradesmen and talking about it at parties. In the middle of the passage, Pope modulates to complete seriousness,

> Why then declare Good-nature is her scorn,
> When 'tis by that alone she can be born?
> Why pique all mortals, yet affect a name?
> A fool to Pleasure, and slave to Fame:

and out again to the sort of social satire which would fit a Congreve play. The passage ends on a chilling aphorism. The whole quotation gives an unforgettable picture of a characteristic woman. It is also as 'beautiful' (and therefore perhaps as 'lyrical') as *Frost at Midnight*, *The Ode to a Nightingale*, the eighth *Pisan Canto* or Gary Snyder among the bears. The beauty of Pope's language must be stressed since it is an overall quality and not a garnishing of intractable material. While theory asserts that no subject is potentially more poetic than another, practice and poets' lack of nerve leads to the habit of adding 'beauty' (usually made up of special lyrical words) to whatever is going on. Pope avoids transcendentalism, and we have grown to expect beauty to have a transcendent aim. *His* aim is to be true to events in the real world but nevertheless to illuminate them by the poet's traditional method—beautiful language, that shining improvement of prosaic statement. The point of his poetry is its justice, strength and memorability. Pope is at home in the fallen world—he does not think we can have Heaven on earth. All we can do is to keep within our limits, but his are the limits of poetry and not of wish-fulfilment.

How serious was Pope's recourse to the Classics?

Pope was privately educated and very well-read. Like Peacock, he read the classics because he loved them and his constant recourse to them in his poetry was not just to lend respectability. Shakespeare had used the classics for their stories (Plutarch, Seneca and Homer—all proverbial stories by this time) but also as modern novelists use the English poets themselves—as suppliers of instantly recognizable examples of universal truths. Pope seems very different: the instances of Homer and the Latin poets are always before his eyes and he claims the ancient authors not as a repository of stories and metaphors but as titans of a golden age whose achievement is unobtainable by any modern author but whose form and decorum must never be forgotten. But they were guides not models. After all, how should the Augustan Englishman copy the primitive Achaean when his life is utterly different and he doesn't even have a verse form in common? The answer could only be by adopting him as a precept. In *The Essay on Criticism*, Pope suggests a reading list of ancient authors (the passage beginning 'Such once were Criticks, such the Happy Few') who guarantee wit, grandeur and common sense. They are all familiar names, from Aristotle to Longinus, and listing them gives Pope the chance to sum up the worth of each in the manner of Quintilian. I suppose the real difficulty with Pope's classicising comes from our doubt of its worth. There are plenty of colleges to supply the learning and annotated editions to explain everything in assimilable form. It is simply that if Pope had not had so firm a grasp of the England of his time, we should have lost patience with his obsession with the classics. His translations themselves make an interesting study of his attitude to the past. His versions of Homer are transformations in a long line of which Pound's *Cantos* are the latest examples. Urban and rational, Pope put the primitive stories of Homer into the most social of English forms, the couplet. Dryden, translating Virgil, was one literary man interpreting another. Pope's versions of *The Iliad* and *The Odyssey* cannot be called successful renderings of Homer but they are monuments to the intelligence of the Western Man-of-letters. Pope shows that he can digest the heroic and reproduce it in very different terms. The Greek expedition to Troy is fabulous but it is also heavy-handed. Pope tames it utterly. A lot has been lost but at least the impossible hasn't been attempted—eighteenth-century man hasn't tried to turn himself into a blood-soaked Achaean. The only modern resource capable of matching the epic is opera, and its flowering came after Pope. What Pope did was remake Homer in the same way that Capability Brown remade the landscape.

From his earliest poems, Pope preferred to use classical figures to dignify modern cases. Sometimes this is no more than giving classical names to English things. But Pope does not confine himself to the Delias, Strephons, Chloes, Amaryllises, etc., of Elizabethan, Caroline and Restoration lyric writers. Mostly, he goes deeper. The classical past (i.e. the thousands of literary and historical persons, gods and places of which Lemprières' Dictionary is the mere catalogue) comes readily into his mind whether he is thinking about Windsor, Grub Street or Lord Hervey. It's true that he could expect his readers to be familiar with his references, but it was not just their universality which appealed to him. If people could be made good by the Imitation of Christ, they could be civilized by the power of the classics. Where today we expect the poet's experience to authenticate his poetry, Pope called on an older and clearer system of values. He was doing no more than the Florentines had done before him, but he had the ancient world in better view and had codified it to his own satisfaction. Centuries of automatic reference by academic writers has no doubt dulled our ears to the classics. Pope's use of them, however, is justified—they lay at the deepest level of his imagination.

Form in Pope

Pope's versification is faultless. The sound of a characteristic Pope passage is as near total euphony as language permits. The only parallel I can find is in Mozart's music; especially Mozart's compositions in his euphonious key, E Flat. Like Mozart's, Pope's perfection can be a little wearing—you start to long for some of the brokenness, willed or unavoidable, of a poet like Browning. Pope's handling of the couplet is never costive, also never emptily virtuoso. He appreciates, as Milton did in the more heavyweight harness of blank verse, that it is syntax which is the key to good poetry. He doesn't pad out lines with adjectives or begin lines too often with conjunctions. His caesuras are nicely placed and his punctuation is dramatic. He was born writing well. The use of the couplet in the *Imitations of Horace* is more daring but not different in kind from its use in the *Essay on Criticism*. Throughout his career, the English language might almost be Italian, the way he handles it—no poetry north of the Alps has ever been so well-fashioned. His supremacy can be demonstrated by comparing his

B

poems with the millions of other lines in couplets, before him and after. Dryden is rougher, Rochester too singular, the many assorted masters of the later eighteenth century too often dull—only Crabbe has a comparable combination of invention and technique, but he has only one view, the realistic. He could never have entered the Cosi-fan-Tutte world of *The Rape of the Lock*.

Pope's perfection of prosody is not matched by his formal ability as an arguer. His major poems are well made in the sense that the verse gives the reader the required sense of inevitability. But he is not a great philosopher and the arguments in even his most tightly constructed poems are episodic and badly balanced. Nevertheless, he remains outwardly loyal to logic. In this he is a true son of his century and the advertisements in front of the poems are proper guides to their subject matter. The purpose of poetry is not philosophy and most people don't notice that *The Essay on Man* leaps all over the place in its compendiousness and that *The Dunciad* is sometimes nonsense. Pope's ground plan for a poem relies on inspiration to maintain momentum. Poems, even social ones, are more like plays than orations—images and persons walk on and delight us and we are won over by the attractiveness of the presentation not by the argument. The same material presented in court would probably lose its case. To consider just one poem in some depth—look at the *Epistle to Allen, Lord Bathurst* on the Use of Riches. Pope lets examples swell beyond their proper dimensions. The apotheosis of the *Man of Ross*, that insipid paternalist, is not only unconvincing but inflated. Nor is there much proportion in the argument up to this point, but a natural progression of poetic ideas lamenting mankind's habit of falling into one of the two extremes, Avarice or Profusion. It is the mean between the two Pope exalts. He surveys his own age,

listing many absurdities arising from the abuse of wealth
—people leaving their money to cats or to sons they hate,
the fear the rich entertain of the poor, the hypocrisy of
the clergy, etc. Behind all these and many other per-
versions lies the one dreadful curse—man's lust for
money.

> But thousands die, without or this or that,
> Die and endow a College, or a Cat:
> To some, indeed, Heav'n grants the happier fate,
> T'enrich a Bastard, or a Son they hate.
> Perhaps you think the Poor might have their part?
> Bond damns the Poor, and hates them from his heart:
> The grave Sir Gilbert holds it for a rule,
> That 'every man in want is knave or fool':
> 'God cannot love (says Blunt, with tearless eyes)
> The wretch he starves'—and piously denies:
> But the good Bishop, with a meeker air,
> Admits, and leaves them, Providence's care.
> Yet, to be just to these poor men of pelf,
> Each does but hate his Neighbour as himself:
> Damn'd to the Mines, an equal fate betides
> The Slave that digs it and the Slave that hides.
> Who suffer thus, mere charity must own,
> Must act on motives powerful, tho' unknown:
> Some War, some Plague, or Famine they foresee,
> Some Revelation hid from you and me.
> Why Shylock wants a meal, the cause is found,
> He thinks a loaf will rise to fifty pound.
> What made Directors cheat in South-Sea year?
> To live on ven'son when it sold so dear.
> Ask you why Phryne the whole Auction buys?
> Phryne foresees a general excise.

It's immediately apparent that the City of Pope's day was
much like it is today. There were monopolies, take-

overs and fraudulent issues. What Pope fears is the destruction of society, the triumph of anarchy. Money is society's cement, so the miser and the profligate equally threaten the security of the state. Pope is serious about this—his moral centre is utilitarian rather than Christian. He is not presuming to lecture Bathurst on how to dispose of his considerable wealth. His purpose is to draw a series of lessons from the unfortunate habits of his day and the practice of antiquity. Moderation for him is not a pallid virtue but a full-blooded one. He hates extremists of all kinds. His poetry attains its greatest power whenever he imagines the disintegration of society, as he does in the final lines of *The Dunciad*. A similar passage occurs in this Third Epistle. It is a vision of the evil wrought by the pursuit of wealth and property.

> At length Corruption, like a gen'ral flood,
> (So long by watchful Ministers withstood)
> Shall deluge all; and Av'rice creeping on,
> Spread like a low-born mist, and blot the Sun;
> Statesman and Patriot ply alike the stocks,
> Peeress and Butler share alike the Box,
> And Judges job, and Bishops bite the town,
> And mighty Dukes pack cards for half a crown.
> See Britain sunk in lucre's sordid charms,
> And France reveng'd of ANNE's and EDWARD's arms!

There must be a hundred other ways of dealing with the effect of money on society. Pope's vision of a collapse is apocalyptic but practical. The insipidity of the *Man of Ross* episode shows that he needed monsters more than angels as every poet does. *The Epistle to Bathurst* is a cry against the black night of anarchy and the misery of a world given over to selfishness; it is more than reasoned Horatian advice offered to a man of the world about how to handle his inheritance. Pope is too passionate to observe his own counsel of moderation or to conduct a wholly fair argument. In the last analysis, we see that form in Pope is inseparable from content.

NOTES ON THE SELECTION OF POEMS

There are some peculiarities in my selection of Pope's poems which require justification. He is at once the hardest and the easiest poet to choose from. On the one hand, he wrote so uniformly well it is difficult to exclude anything on the ground of its failing to come up to standard; on the other, he is a poet of major works, so that it should be easy to decide which five or six of them are the most important and merely reprint those. I have adopted a strange and middle course. The only poems reproduced entire are *The Second Moral Essay* or *Epistle to a Lady* and the *Epistle to Dr. Arbuthnot*. I have included only the last three cantos of *The Rape of the Lock* and only the second epistle of the *Essay on Man*. And again I have truncated *The Essay on Criticism* by some two hundred lines. I apologize for the eccentricity of selecting only one part of *The Essay on Man*. It is a masterpiece, of course, but there are things I prefer to promote in Pope's work and the poem is perhaps the best known of all his major productions. In justification of the other unorthodox pieces of editing, I refer back to my earlier remarks about the continuity of any major Pope poem. While the verse is seamless, I find the argument is not; and I have been tempted to dissect the long poems into passages of extraordinary excellence, where the poet has taken wing and produced self-contained masterpieces. I'm sorry to have maltreated so superb a poem as *The Essay on Criticism* in this way, but feel on surer ground with the other edited works. *The Dunciad* is perhaps as over-valued today as once it was underrated (I have an 1826 popular edition of Pope which says simply that *The Dunciad* 'has long been laid aside'). Pope's argument in *The Dunciad* is straightforward in general purpose and impossibly labyrinthine in detail. Also the poem's change of hero from Theobald to Cibber when the three-canto edition became the 1742 four-canto one doesn't make for clarity. Instead of taking the easy way out and quoting only Canto Four, which is certainly the best, I have lopped out parts from all over the poem. I hope I have not therefore produced a book which might be called 'gems from Pope'. Each extract from whatever poem makes sense by itself, and more importantly, is, to my ear, *poetically satisfying* in its isolation. One other point of choice should be accounted for—there is nothing from his translations of *The Iliad* and *The Odyssey*. These were almost half his life's work in duration and more than that in number of lines. And they are remarkable enough as poetry. In defence of my decision to exclude them, I quote what Pope wrote of his own hard labour—

> While Wren with sorrow to the grave descends,
> Gay dies unpensioned with a hundred friends,
> Hibernian politics, O Swift, thy fate;
> And Pope's, ten years to comment and translate.

His Homer and his Shakespeare editions were remarkable and made him money but they were not his first choice of work. His genius was satirical in the largest meaning of that term and while I would rather read Homer in Pope's couplets than in anyone's fustian, I think the two poets are not well matched. The shorter and slighter poems included are there to correct the picture of Pope as lengthy and serious. I like light verse: I even like poetical squibs, and Pope and Swift wrote many. *Eloisa and Abelard*, *Messiah* and *Epistle to Miss Blount* are missing. Besides being over-celebrated, they are readily available in general anthologies.

I have dispensed with line numbering in the margin, as this seemed pointless when reproducing only extracts from a poem, and I have included Pope's own prose advertisement at the beginning of a poem only when printing the whole poem or when it was essential for an understanding of the work. This brings me to the most vexed of problems for the editor of a selection of Pope intended for a popular market. Should there be footnotes to explain the hundreds of contemporary references— not merely the originals disguised by classical sobriquets, but the very meaning of certain passages which time and history have obscured? The magnificent Twickenham edition is available (at a great price or in a library) to explain everything, but even the one-volume Twickenham includes pretty copious notes. Half-regretfully, I have decided against a clutter of small type at the foot of the page. What I am hoping is that people will get into the habit of reading Pope with that onward movement which his versification is scored for. It is dispiriting to follow some half-dozen iambic lines at the top of a dense silt of prose. But to make the most important points plain there follows here a brief set of notes on the poems in this selection.

Summer. *The Second Pastoral*

Very enamelled verse in which the young poet establishes both his orthodoxy and his matchless ease of versifying. Under the Virgilian surface, England is recognizable. This is an early example of the concealed realism of Pope. Dr. Samuel Garth, author of *The Dispensary*, befriended Pope when the poet was only in his teens. Apart from Virgil, Spenser is recalled. Pope says that the scene of this pastoral is by the river's side and the time is noon. It is surprising how mixed, not to say impure, the material of neo-classical writing can be. Whether Pope enjoyed having Handel set his lines beginning 'Where-e'er you walk' is not known. His attitude to music is hardly friendly, unlike Dryden's. When he praises it, he means the mellifluous or musical effect of correct sound in poetry.

An Essay on Criticism

This poem may be a compendium of received ideas but it is possibly the most remarkable piece of precocity in English. It was written in 1709, when Pope was twenty-one and it is designed less to keep the reader's nose in the classics than to be the opening campaign in Pope's war against Dullness and Bad Judging. Invention is his watch-word and we shouldn't overestimate the weight of the classics or neglect his respect for good sense. References to his own society are as numerous as to the classical past. Maro is Virgil; the Stagyrite is Aristotle, and Longinus was the famous Hellenistic critic from Palmyra, etc. The contrast or war between ancient and modern authors had been a popular subject ever since Martial and Plutarch. Perrault and Swift turned to the theme in Pope's time. Nothing arcane is needed however to understand Pope's general argument. Fungoso, for instance, is a character in Ben Jonson's *Every Man in His Humour*, but the point about showing-off can be taken without knowing this. My advice is to be guided by the joke about the Presbyterian preacher who when confronted by difficulties of theology, simply went round them. Duck Lane is where old and second-hand books were sold. Dionysius of Halicarnassus was one of the most famous commentators on Homer and Quintilian the Roman orator who gave his name to the art of summing up literary excellence in a nutshell: Pope and he had much in common and Pope has recourse to his

24

works often. *Leo's Golden Days* is a tribute to the Medicean Pope Leo XII's patronage of great Renaissance artists, such as Raphael and Michelangelo. Those who do not know the classics will remain in ignorance of Pope's parallels with Ovid, Virgil and others; likewise the proper names of his own time will be mysterious. The solution is not to substitute appropriate persons from our civilization but to enjoy the names for their own sake. The origin of poetry was naming. *An Essay on Criticism* is witty and accessible to anybody who reads good literature. A brief note on Pope's prosody. 'Heav'n' is always scanned as a single syllable. All such unsounded vowels as the second 'e' in 'Heav'n' are marked by an apostrophe in the text. Printed vowels are to be sounded, though they carry no accent—such as 'winged' in the line 'The winged Courser, like a gen'rous Horse.' This line illustrates Pope's convention of sounded and unsounded 'e's'. He almost never writes an irregular iambic line, though he is not quite so absolute about rhyming, where imperfections should not all be attributed to changes in pronunciation since the eighteenth century.

The Temple of Fame

Early on, Pope wrote some imitations of the English poets which were mere exercises (though they were so good I have included two in this selection). But the principle of parody was one he followed throughout his life. Parody should be understood in the musical sense— i.e. basing a new work on the structure, material but not usually the tone or feeling of an earlier model. But this piece is not much like Chaucer, while the Horace and Donne re-workings keep a lot of the original. It is an allegory of a fairly simple sort—a medieval dream of the true and the false. The passage included here is the climax of the poem where the aspirant to fame is shown the tumultuous citadel itself and the hazards which surround it. At a low level, the moral is that ambition misleads more men than it inspires, but Pope believes there is a serious Pantheon where the immortals are enshrined.

Windsor Forest

The most obviously English of Pope's pastorals. The whole of rural England is shaped by man and Windsor Forest is appropriately enough described from the point of view of an eighteenth-century town-dweller. It should be borne in mind that the Augustan view of nature is hardly different from Beethoven's in his Pastoral Symphony or even painters such as Caspar David Friedrich—i.e. the picturesque is esteemed as well as the classic. This was also the manner of the Roman poets if not quite of Theocritus. Midway between natural science and human sententiousness, Pope is as didactic as ever and celebrates British arms and Imperial expansion. The check-list of rivers is imitated from the classics but inspires Pope to one of his most magnificent pieces of rhetoric. He sees the liberalizing influence of Britain in traditional terms— for instance in opposition to the tyrannical Spanish with their fondness for breaking people on the wheel and maltreating the South American Indians. Windsor Forest was to London what the Wiener Wald was to Beethoven's Vienna, and so it is appropriate that this pastoral should include an encomium of London. There seem no great difficulties in the text—a visit to the dictionary or encyclopaedia will cover most of the unfamiliar names. Augusta was the Roman name for London. The Vandalis is the river Wandle. 'The Ister's foaming Flood' is the Danube, nearby which Marlborough (a Whig and not of Pope's party) won his great victory of Blenheim.

I find the war for the recovery of Helen which destroyed Troy a good deal more ridiculous than the mock hostilities which ensue after Belinda's curl is snipped off. This heroi-comical mini-epic is its poet's most finished and perfect work. Where Homer's and Virgil's gods take sides in the realistic battles of their epics, so Pope's sylphs and creatures of the air buzz about the upsets of a fashionable lady's social day. Pope is not satirizing the epics, he is finding the right parody-form for a poem on the intrinsic order of life. As Freud pointed out, civilization is the one thing man has to be proud of. Nobody believed in it more passionately than Pope and wrote more convincingly in its defence. Likewise, Pope defended the things he loved—the classics and the classical order of life—by making the rational sublime and preventing the fantastic from becoming absurd (the tragic case of individual inspiration running riot in English verse being William Blake). We need not bother to note the parallels with epic poetry in *The Rape of the Lock* any more than in Joyce's *Ulysses*. The first two cantos describe Belinda's toilet and introduce her protective spirits. The curls of hair are as dear to her and her train as the beauty and prestige of Helen were to the Trojans. The Baron who would add one of these locks to his collection of ladies' favours is presented in his turn as a supplicant to fate for the success of his intended rape. Now read on, as the serials say. The action of the poem is not complex (card game, rape, ensuing battle and final assumption of the Lock into Heaven to dwell among the constellations), though the beautifully light use of hyperbole needs to be taken in at several and not just one reading. The opening of Canto Three is one of Pope's most familiar passages. The equivalents of the ritualized fights among the heroes beneath the walls of Troy are society's beloved card games and the *Iliad* parody is very close. This being mock-heroic, all the bigs become littles but the triumph of the Baron's rape is in exactly the same high language as it would be if he were Hector. It is only the object which is different. The rape of the lock brings its lament and consequent revenge—this is the high point of the poem. Pope heaps mock violence upon mock violence and we are offered a world of total transformation; metamorphoses quainter than Ovid's accrue until society itself is seen at complete variance with its own decorums. The parody here may even extend to Shakespeare's view of order as outlined in Odysseus's speech in *Troilus and Cressida*. What Pope sees as deplorable anarchy in the *Epistle to Bathurst* and *The Dunciad* is here done lightly and turned into a sublime comic-strip or Lewis Carroll dream. Four of my favourite lines in English literature occur in this section and I cannot resist quoting them—the first two from Canto Four—

> Men prove with Child, as powerful Fancy works,
> And Maids turn'd Bottles, call aloud for Corks.

and the second from the final canto—

> A *Beau* and *Witling* perished in the *Th*rong,
> One dy'd in *Metaphor*, and one in *Song*.

Most of the classical personages in the poem can be looked-up in Lemprière's dictionary. Those thumb-nail biographies will be enough to follow Pope's use of them in the poem. If the imitations of specific speeches from Homer aren't recognized, it will not be a serious loss. The great tenderness which Pope had for people of good will is very evident in the poem, as is also his fantastic imagination. This mannered mock-epic turns out to be his most natural poem and the one which illustrates most clearly his divine good humour.

A Farewell to London

A genial piece of light verse. The people named are all writer-friends, patrons, booksellers, politicians and Grub Street denizens. Perhaps the tone is not quite natural to Pope—he isn't usually so clubable—but it is nicely done. It is more a Restoration poem in the Sedley/Rochester mode.

Verses Occassion'd by an Etc. at the End of Mr. D'Urfy's Name

A joke but well carried out. This poem joins hands across the years with the modern game-and-joke poems of Christopher Middleton, George MacBeth and even Robert Graves. Pope tells us in a note that Neufgermain was a poet who used to make verses ending with the last syllables of the names of persons he praised.

The Gulliver Poems

Pope, Swift, Gay and Arbuthnot had an affection for each other which extended beyond the Scriblerus Club. These graceful variations on *Gulliver's Travels* are equivalent to the musical modifications which Bach was playing upon Telemann and Vivaldi. Glumdalclitch is the young Brobdingnagian girl who looked after Gulliver at the Court, and Grildrig was her familiar name for him. Pope's admiration for Swift went deeper than friendship: there was no other writer he would have put beside himself.

An Essay on Man

Pope intended this famous poem as the first part of a much greater enterprise, to be 'a general Map of Man'. *The Moral Essays*, *The Epistle to Dr. Arbuthnot* and the variously entitled pieces imitated from Horace make up a poetical compendium of the Universal Laws of Humanity. The ambition is enormous and the only flaw that can be discovered in the execution is the necessary one that poetry is not philosophy. Pope says he chose verse deliberately because precepts are better remembered in poetical form and because poetical arguments are more concise. Nevertheless, we read these works for their *poetry* and while they are studded with passages which are now proverbial in English, they cannot be considered great philosophy. *The Essay on Man* together with the earlier *Essay on Criticism* is responsible for Pope's bad reputation as a regurgitator of the received ideas of his day. T. S. Eliot, lamenting Blake, argued that a poet was the better for adhering to some fixed system of belief. It isn't just a matter of writing 'what oft was thought but ne'er so well expressed'. The greatest genius in poetry lies in making the familiar sublime, and Pope does so continuously. The principle of a Predominant or Ruling Passion is a very eighteenth-century idea. We wear our liberalism differently but the return of Adlerian ideas to psychology may yet make Pope's old-fashioned concept real to us. As always the resolution of extremes in a middle way was what appealed to Pope (see his advice on the Use of Riches). Whether his didacticism is applicable in practice is doubtful. There is some truth in the modern view that human beings, even if not incorrigible, aren't much moved by good arguments. To avoid a slight feeling of smugness, it is advisable to read *The Essay on Man* in conjunction with its neighbouring epistles. The debt to Rochester's *A Satire against Mankind* is quite pronounced —viz., the famous lines from Rochester,

> Huddled in dirt, the reas'ning Engine lies,
> Who was so proud, so witty, and so wise.

Moral Essays. Epistle II. To a Lady

The lady is Martha Blount, perhaps Pope's mistress or wife and a Catholic and life-long friend. In my opinion this is the best poem Pope ever wrote and one which needs little explanation. He may be harsh with women but he doesn't excoriate them as Juvenal does in his Sixth Satire, nor find their animal natures coarser than men's, like Swift (though Swift should not be saddled with a pathological distaste for women. His scabrous poems are more playful than that). A few technical notes may be in order. 'Rufa studying Locke' is particularly ridiculous if you credit red-haired women with being more lubricious than others and so less likely to bother with political economy. Sappho here is Lady Mary Wortley Montagu. Taylor is Jeremy Taylor, author of that popular and uplifting book, *Holy Living and Holy Dying*. 'Caesar and Tall-Boy, Charles and Charlema'ne' is the contrast between Emperor and Servant. Chartres was the most notorious rogue of the day whose death was celebrated in a fine vituperative epitaph by Dr. Arbuthnot. He comes back in *The Epistle to Bathurst*. Helluo is Latin for glutton. Ratafie is a liqueur-like drink. Pope's Atossa was the Duchess of Buckinghamshire with whom he had a long record of disagreements. What they were is not of consequence since the personality of such a woman of extremes repeats itself in nature. So too with Cloe—whoever she was, most of us have a woman like her in our acquaintance or, more unhappily, in our lives. The Duchess of Queensberry was famous for her beauty. The Ring was the favourite carriage-ride in Hyde Park. Miss Blount must have been an agreeable person to have received so attractive a tribute from the poet. I suspect people mistake Pope's deformity and misanthropy. This poem suggests, at least, he was no misogynist.

Epistle III. To Allen Lord Bathurst

The subject is the proper use of riches. I have discussed this poem at an earlier point in the Introduction and will just supply a few notes here. Worldly is Lady Mary

Wortley Montagu's husband and all the examples here are of businessmen or noblemen, either trying for a quick profit or losing their fortunes through follies at the gaming tables. White's is the chocolate house which became a gentleman's club. Uxorio is Lord Hervey. It's sad that Pope had such an aversion to this remarkable man and his patroness, Queen Caroline. Posterity can afford to admire the way both men wrote. Quadrille was one of the fashionable card games. *Imp'd* means feathered, a device of adding plumes in falconry. Turner was a man like Shaw's Millionairess, to whom the loss of any small sum was as painful as the princess's pea beneath her mattresses—a truly sensitive miser, in fact. Wharton was unfortunate in his investments; Hopkins was known as 'Vulture' Hopkins; Chartres cheated and denied everybody and was proverbial for cupidity; Japhet Crook, being convicted of fraud, had his nose and ears lopped off in the public stocks. It is worth reflecting on the realities which lay behind the Augustan calm, and considering whether our cut-price car-insurance men and take-over kings would consider the risk worth the candle. The original Narses was the eunuch of Justinian's Court who turned general after Belisarius's death and defeated the Goths. He stands here for the first Earl of Cadogan, who presumably had piles or some ailment like Sulla's described by Plutarch. Freud and others have pointed to the symbolical links between faeces and money, and sphincters and credit. The ailments come accordingly. People *do* leave their money to cats. My own father considered the cause of sick racehorses. Sir Gilbert and his friends in the City are still with us—this is the worst part of the Protestant Ethic. It's convenient to believe that poverty arises from weakness or idleness. The South Sea Bubble was a famous city scandal when the share issue (see Poseidon in 1970) raised commodity prices ridiculously before paper credit collapsed. Phryne, the Athenian courtesan who made a fortune, indicates Walpole's mistress. Women have always been good at managing the money affairs of their consorts. The list of these money men becomes as tedious as the financial pages of our own newspapers. The poem from this point on is a magnificent piece of forensic argument (see Introduction).

An Epistle from Mr. Pope, to Dr. Arbuthnot

In addition to being Pope's second most perfect poem, this has the character of a confession. Here Pope goes some way to disclosing his nature and temperament. Of course, it is ostensibly a private letter, but Arbuthnot was known to the audience as Pope's close friend and all that passed between him and Pope was intended to be marked and noted. The bitterness against Grub Street intriguers is fair enough—Pope had been plagued a great deal and often for no better reason than that his writings brought him fame. Also, he was much applied to by aspirant authors and their doting parents. His most prominent enemies come under censure here—Walpole and Queen Caroline, Lord Hervey, Colly Cibber, Ambrose Philips and the rest. They tend to be remembered today only because of Pope's enmity towards them. The bad corollary of this is that we in our turn think of Pope as a bitter and contumacious person. Certainly, he was not bland and never spoke in the undifferentiated terms of good will common today but the fault of his severity is more to be laid at the door of his century and his society. There were no libel laws and a man could print not only what he liked but what was of advantage to him. At least Pope could claim that his dislikes were his own. He was never a party hack and some of the resentment which fills this poem and overflows in *The Dunciad* was due to his coming under attack for reasons of faction. Naturally he felt contempt for opponents whose polemic was merely bought. 'Ammon's great Son' was Alexander the Great, and immediately after this reference we come to Pope's own account of his calling to his craft. The oracle of Jupiter Ammon had spoken for the first great Alexander and his English name-sharer is identifying with him.

> I left no Calling for this idle trade,
> No Duty broke, no Father dis-obey'd.
> The Muse but serv'd to ease some Friend, not Wife,
> To help me thro' this long Disease, my Life.

These are the most modest and yet most assertive lines I know and shame the mystics who think poetry should usurp the task of religion. As always, Pope's categories are beautifully in place. Slashing Bentley was the poor fellow who thought he knew better than Milton what Milton meant to write. Critics are seldom so brave, preferring to cavil. The portrait of Addison—'Peace to all such! but were there One whose fires' etc.—had been written years before and Pope denied that his attack was made only post-humously. It seems in all particulars, fair. Addison was the originator of 'smooth' judging. In his elevation of the craft of belles-lettres or the Senior Common Room Code of Good Taste, Addison has much to answer for —as well as his way of making English prose so melli-fluous, not to say emulsified. We may think, without be-ing too wise after the event, that he deserved Pope's hard portrait of him. Sporus is Lord Hervey. The reader is referred to Hervey's own journals of his time at George II's Court for a balancing view of his character. He is a most polished writer of English prose. It is very hard to recapture the venom of eighteenth-century faction and Hervey's opposition to Pope and his friends was un-doubtedly vicious. Just or unjust, *The Epistle to Arbuthnot* is Pope's most moving poem. A career in letters, even with noblemen and geniuses for friends and the consolations of so attractive a retreat as Pope's at Twickenham, could be heart-breaking. This poem is Pope's equivalent to the *Lines on the Death of Dr. Swift*.

The First Epistle of the Second Book of Horace Imitated

Horace has always been the Englishman's favourite Latin poet and the Horatian tone (a level but elevated combination of good sense and imagination) suited Pope admirably. Pope wrote his Horace and Donne imitations as a direct result of the furore caused by his earlier epistles. The advertisement to the *Imitations* included these words. 'An answer from Horace was both more full, and of more Dignity, than any I cou'd have made in my own person; and the Example of much greater Freedom in so eminent a Divine as Dr. Donne, seem'd a proof with what Indignation and Contempt a Christian may treat Vice or Folly. . . .' *The First Epistle of the Second Book* was dedicated to the Emperor Augustus by Horace. Pope is at pains to draw attention to Horace's lack of servility towards his Emperor. His argument goes—'this Piece . . . was an Apology for the Poets, in order to render Augustus more their Patron. Horace here pleads the cause of his Contemporaries, first against the Taste of the Town, whose humour it was to magnify the Authors of the preceding Age; secondly against the Court and Nobility, who encouraged only the Writers for the Theatre; and lastly against the Emperor himself, who had conceived them of little use to the Government. . . . We may further learn from this Epistle, that Horace made his Court to this Great Prince, by writing with a decent Freedom toward him, with a just Contempt towards his low Flatterers, and with manly regard to his own Character.' Since Pope's Augustus, King George II, disliked literature and trusted Sir Robert Walpole, who ruled by bribes and flattery, Pope was more ironical than reverent in his dedication. The passages I have extracted from the poem are interesting as Pope's judgments of his poetical predecessors and of his taste in literary matters generally. Some of his views are unexpected—he is by no means always on the side of the ancients against the moderns.

> I lose my patience, and I own it too,
> When works are censur'd, not as bad, but new;

and a little later on

> Had ancient Times conspir'd to dis-allow
> What then was new, what had been ancient now?

Taking our taste and habits from France was as common then as it is today. The second of the two extracts pursues the familiar argument that our native drama, though lacking the polish of the French, may surpass it in energy and invention. But Pope had the poet's ambiguity towards the theatre where the mob judges rather than the man of taste. (Who among today's poets, reflecting on his small fame and bank balance, doesn't cast an envious eye on Pinter, Osborne, Stoppard and company and wonder if they are the fine artists their numerous admirers take them for?) This whole version of Horace is very partial judging in literary terms.

The Second Epistle of the Second Book of Horace Imitated

I have selected only a short self-contained passage from this extensive poem. As a recipe for the writing of good verse it is admirably practical.

The Seventh Epistle of the First Book of Horace

When Pope announces that his poem will be in the style of Swift, you may be sure that the imitation will be exact. The commonsense tone, with its ability to leap from the ordinary to the striking in one line, is as characteristic of the Dean's manner as the choice of octosyllabics instead of decasyllabics. Craggs and Child were two men of consequence and Pope's benefactors. Harley was Earl of Oxford and a lifelong friend of the Poet.

Donne's Fourth Satire, Versifyed

Modern taste asks tartly whether Donne's original wasn't already versified. But Pope meant that he had smoothed out the irregularities of Elizabethan prosody as well as having brought the instances up to date. We don't feel much sympathy for endeavours of this sort: our imitations go the other way, making the plain places rough. But a comparison of the lines I have chosen with the equivalent lines of Donne (lines 188 onwards) shows some advantages to Pope. He has made it all clearer, if less idiosyncratic. The opening lines of each make a fair comparison:

Donne:

 The Ladies come; As Pirats, which doe know
 That there came weak ships fraught with Cutchannel,
 The men board them; and praise, as they thinke, well,
 Their beauties; they the mens wits; Both are bought.

Pope:

 Painted for sight, and essenc'd for the smell,
 Like Frigates fraught with Spice and Cochine'l,
 Sail in the *Ladies*: How each Pyrate eyes
 So weak a Vessel, and so rich a Prize!

Donne's punctuation and syntax is marvellous—it's dramatic in the extreme. But it's a bit out of focus. Pope, in making the point easier to follow, has lost Donne's ability to find drama within the five feet of one line. On the other hand, Pope gets the better of it by his beautiful delaying of the ladies' entrance, so that the first word of

37

the third line is truly under full sail. The comparison is unfair, of course—Pope, in expanding the original, is working at different rhyme points and therefore one cannot compare identical sets of couplets. I think this poem (and the extract I've chosen) should be read for the rare pleasure of observing the second greatest poet in English re-working the verses of the third greatest. If you don't like categories, you can still enjoy the poem.

The Dunciad

W. H. Auden remarks that to have seen Dullness, the goddess of minor and in themselves unimportant figures, as a really formidable and eternal threat to the City of Man was a vision in its own way as original and of as permanent value to the City as Dante's of Paradise or Wordsworth's of Nature. To which, Amen. But *The Dunciad* is a very quixotic poem. It started off in Pope's reaction to the scholars' attacks on his edition of Shakespeare and the envy his talents aroused in rivals. It became, both in the earlier form with Theobald as Chief Dunce and in the later version with Cibber as hero, Pope's equivalent to *The Battle of the Books*, At this distance in time, it behoves modern readers to esteem Pope and Swift not because they were maintaining the true standards of antiquity against the dunces and hacks of Grub Street, but because they wrote so much better. Both sides freely called on the past to be their witness. Auden also advises reading the poem without notes and substituting contemporary fools for the eighteenth-century ones. But you can't do this if you don't know which are which. The only course with *The Dunciad* is to read it two ways, several times each. First tear through it like an express and relish the speed of its rhetoric. Then read it in a properly annotated edition and consult each footnote as it occurs. Meanwhile, regard the extracts here as samplers. *The Dunciad* is to Pope's whole canon what late and difficult plays like *Cymbeline* and *Timon* are to Shakespeare. Not only is the matter strange, the poetry is utterly audacious. Pope never turned the couplet to weirder uses than in this anti-epic. His imagination becomes grotesque, he sees a world dislocated from its classic order by a whole horde of ambitious suitors to Dullness. She is a goddess he takes seriously. Her kingdom on earth is to be tasteless, unquiet, extensive and eternal. If he could see modern Europe he might think the day of her triumph had come. I give up with relief any attempt to annotate even the passages which I have chosen to reproduce. One guide line is—don't be too impressed by the 'iad' ending. Whereas *The Rape of the Lock* is a true mock-epic, this is more like *The Vision of Piers Plowman*. Pope will whirl you through the psychedelic mixtures of his awful vision of anarchy. It's a bad trip, but in the most splendid language. The final lines of the Goddess's triumph are among the most celebrated in the English language. They answer all critics' questions as to whether you can make boring subjects interesting in art. The vision is Dantesque. *The Dunciad* is too long and too bizarre to be Pope's greatest work. It remains, however, his most outrageous masterpiece.

Epigrams, Etc.

I preferred all of these to the famous Epitaph on Newton. The disagreeable piece on Queen Caroline is to make up for overestimating Pope's good will. He could be vicious to his enemies. This couplet is an unjust reflection on the death-bed of a woman who suffered with great fortitude.

Summer. *The Second Pastoral, or Alexis*

TO DR. GARTH

A Shepherd's Boy (he seeks no better Name)
Let forth his Flocks along the silver *Thame*,
Where dancing Sun-beams on the Waters play'd,
And verdant Alders form'd a quiv'ring Shade.
Soft as he mourn'd, the Streams forgot to flow,
The Flocks around a dumb Compassion show,
The *Naiads* wept in ev'ry Watry Bow'r,
And *Jove* consented in a silent Show'r.

   Accept, O *Garth*, the Muse's early Lays,
That adds this Wreath of Ivy to thy Bays;
Hear what from Love unpractis'd Hearts endure,
From Love, the sole Disease thou canst not cure!

   Ye shady Beeches, and ye cooling Streams,
Defence from *Phoebus*', not from *Cupid's* Beams;
To you I mourn; nor to the Deaf I sing,
The Woods shall answer, and their Echo ring.
The Hills and Rocks attend my doleful Lay,
Why art thou prouder and more hard than they?
The bleating Sheep with my Complaints agree,
They parch'd with Heat, and I inflam'd by thee.
The sultry *Sirius* burns the thirsty Plains,
While in thy Heart Eternal Winter reigns.

   Where stray ye Muses, in what Lawn or Grove,
While your *Alexis* pines in hopeless Love?
In those fair Fields where Sacred *Isis* glides,
Or else where *Cam* his winding Vales divides?
As in the Crystal Spring I view my Face,
Fresh rising Blushes paint the watry Glass;
But since those Graces please thy Eyes no more,
I shun the Fountains which I sought before.
Once I was skill'd in ev'ry Herb that grew,

And ev'ry Plant that drinks the Morning Dew;
Ah wretched Shepherd, what avails thy Art,
To cure thy Lambs, but not to heal thy Heart!
    Let other Swains attend the Rural Care,
Feed fairer Flocks, or richer Fleeces share;
But nigh yon' Mountain let me tune my Lays,
Embrace my Love, and bind my Brows with Bays.
That Flute is mine which *Colin*'s tuneful Breath
Inspir'd when living, and bequeath'd in Death;
He said; *Alexis*, take this Pipe, the same
That taught the Groves my *Rosalinda*'s Name—
But now the Reeds shall hang on yonder Tree,
For ever silent, since despis'd by thee.
O were I made by some transforming Pow'r,
The Captive Bird that sings within thy Bow'r!
Then might my Voice thy lis t'ning Ears employ,
And I those Kisses he receives, enjoy.
    And yet my Numbers please the rural Throng,
Rough *Satyrs* dance, and *Pan* applauds the Song:
The Nymphs forsaking ev'ry Cave and Spring,
Their early Fruit, and milk-white Turtles bring;
Each am'rous Nymph prefers her Gifts in vain,
On you their Gifts are all bestow'd again!
For you the Swains the fairest Flow'rs design,
And in one Garland all their Beauties join;
Accept the Wreath which You deserve alone,
In whom all Beauties are compriz'd in One.
    See what Delights in Sylvan Scenes appear!
Descending Gods have found *Elysium* here.
In Woods bright *Venus* with *Adonis* stray'd,
And chast *Diana* haunts the Forest Shade.
Come lovely Nymph, and bless the silent Hours,
When Swains from Sheering seek their nightly Bow'rs;
When weary Reapers quit the sultry Field,
And crown'd with Corn, their Thanks to *Ceres* yield.

This harmless Grove no lurking Viper hides,
But in my Breast the Serpent Love abides.
Here Bees from Blossoms sip the rosie Dew,
But your *Alexis* knows no Sweets but you.
Oh deign to visit our forsaken Seats,
The mossie Fountains, and the Green Retreats!
Where-e'er you walk, cool Gales shall fan the Glade,
Trees, where you sit, shall crowd into a Shade,
Where-e'er you tread, the blushing Flow'rs shall rise,
And all things flourish where you turn your Eyes.
Oh! how I long with you to pass my Days,
Invoke the Muses, and resound your Praise;
Your praise the Birds shall chant in ev'ry Grove,
And Winds shall waft it to the Pow'rs above.
But wou'd you sing, and rival *Orpheus'* Strain,
The wondring Forests soon shou'd dance again,
The moving Mountains hear the pow'rful Call,
And headlong Streams hang list'ning in their Fall!

But see, the Shepherds shun the Noon-day Heat,
The lowing Herds to murm'ring Brooks retreat,
To closer Shades the panting Flocks remove,
Ye Gods! and is there no Relief for Love?
But soon the Sun with milder Rays descends
To the cool Ocean, where his Journey ends;
On me Love's fiercer Flames for every prey,
By night he scorches, as he burns by Day.

An Essay on Criticism

——————————Si quid novisti rectius istis,
Candidus imperti ; si non, his utere mecum.
HORAT.

EXTRACTS

(lines 68–180)

First follow NATURE, and your Judgment frame
By her just Standard, which is still the same:
Unerring Nature, still divinely bright,
One *clear*, *unchang'd*, and *Universal* Light,
Life, Force, and Beauty, must to all impart,
At once the *Source*, and *End*, and *Test* of *Art*.
Art from that Fund each *just Supply* provides,
Works *without Show*, and *without Pomp* presides:
In some fair Body thus th' informing Soul
With Spirits feeds, with Vigour fills the whole,
Each Motion guides, and ev'ry Nerve sustains;
It self unseen, but in th' *Effects*, remains.
Some, to whom Heav'n in Wit has been profuse,
Want as much more, to turn it to its use;
For *Wit* and *Judgment* often are at strife,
Tho' meant each other's Aid, like *Man* and *Wife*.
'Tis more to *guide* than *spur* the Muse's Steed;
Restrain his Fury, than provoke his Speed;
The winged Courser, like a gen'rous Horse,
Shows most true Mettle when you *check* his Course.
Those RULES of old *discover'd*, not *devis'd*,
Are *Nature* still, but *Nature Methodiz'd*;
Nature, like *Liberty*, is but restrain'd
By the same Laws which first *herself* ordain'd.
Hear how learn'd *Greece* her useful Rules indites,
When to repress, and when indulge our Flights:

44

High on *Parnassus*' Top her Sons she show'd,
And pointed out those arduous Paths they trod,
Held from afar, aloft, th' Immortal Prize,
And urg'd the rest by equal Steps to rise;
Just *Precepts* thus from great *Examples* giv'n,
She drew from *them* what they deriv'd from *Heav'n*.
The gen'rous Critick *fann'd* the *Poet's Fire*,
And taught the World, *with Reason* to *Admire*.
Then Criticism the Muse's Handmaid prov'd,
To dress her Charms, and make her more belov'd;
But following Wits from that Intention stray'd;
Who cou'd not win the Mistress, woo'd the Maid;
Against the Poets *their own Arms* they turn'd,
Sure to hate most the Men from whom they *learn'd*.
So modern *Pothecaries*, taight the Art
By *Doctor's Bills* to play the *Doctor's Part*,
Bold in the Practice of *mistaken Rules*,
Prescribe, apply, and call their *Masters Fools*.
Some on the Leaves of ancient Authors prey,
Nor Time nor Moths e'er spoil'd so much as they:
Some dryly plain, without Invention's Aid,
Write dull *Receits* how Poems may be made: *Recipe*
These leave the Sense, their Learning to display,
And those explain the Meaning quite away.
    You then whose Judgment the right Course wou'd
        steer,
Know well each ANCIENT's proper *Character*,
His *Fable, Subject, Scope* in ev'ry Page,
Religion, Country, Genius of his *Age*:
Without all these at once before your Eyes,
Cavil you may, but never *Criticize*.
Be *Homer's* Works your *Study*, and *Delight*,
Read them by Day, and meditate by Night,
Thence form your Judgment, thence your Maxims bring,
And trace the Muses *upward* to their *Spring*;

Still with *It self compar'd*, his *Text* peruse;
And let your *Comment* be the *Mantuan Muse*.
　　When first young *Maro* in his boundless Mind
A Work t' outlast Immortal *Rome* design'd,
Perhaps he seem'd *above* the Critick's Law,
And but from *Nature's Fountains* scorn'd to draw:
But when t'examine ev'ry Part he came,
Nature and *Homer* were, he found, the *same*:
Convinc'd, amaz'd, he checks the bold Design, ⎫
And Rules as strict his labour'd Work confine, ⎬
As if the *Stagyrite* o'erlook'd each Line. ⎭
Learn hence for Ancient *Rules* a just Esteem;
To copy *Nature* is to copy *Them*.
　　Some Beauties yet, no Precepts can declare,
For there's a *Happiness* as well as *Care*.
Musick resembles *Poetry*, in each ⎫
Are *nameless Graces* which no Methods teach, ⎬
And which a *Master-Hand* alone can reach. ⎭
If, where the *Rules* not far enough extend,
(Since Rules were made but to promote their End)
Some Lucky LICENCE answers to the full
Th' Intent propos'd, *that Licence is a Rule.*
Thus *Pegasus*, a nearer way to take,
May boldly deviate from the common Track.
Great Wits sometimes may *gloriously offend*,
And *rise* to *Faults* true Criticks *dare not mend*;
From *vulgar Bounds* with *brave Disorder* part,
And *snatch* a *Grace* beyond the Reach of Art,
Which, without passing thro' the *Judgment*, gains
The *Heart*, and all its End *at once* attains.
In *Prospects*, thus, some *Objects* please our Eyes, ⎫
Which *out of* Nature's *common Order* rise, ⎬
The shapeless *Rock*, or hanging *Precipice*. ⎭
But tho' the *Ancients* thus their *Rules* invade,
(As *Kings* dispense with *Laws* Themselves have made)

46

Moderns, beware! Or if you must offend
Against the *Precept*, ne'er transgress its *End*,
Let it be *seldom*, and *compell'd by Need*,
And have, at least, *Their Precedent* to plead.
The Critick else proceeds without Remorse,
Seizes your Fame, and puts his Laws in force.
   I know there are, to whose presumptuous
      Thoughts
Those *Freer Beauties*, ev'n in *Them*, seem Faults:
Some Figures *monstrous* and *mis-shap'd* appear,
Consider'd *singly*, or beheld too *near*,
Which, but *proportion'd* to their *Light*, or *Place*,
Due Distance *reconciles* to Form and Grace.
A prudent Chief not always must display
His Pow'rs in *equal Ranks*, and *fair Array*,
But with th' *Occasion* and the *Place* comply,
Conceal his Force, nay seem sometimes to *Fly*.
Those oft are *Stratagems* which *Errors* seem,
Nor is it *Homer Nods*, but *We* that *Dream*.

       (lines 233–266)
   A perfect Judge will *read* each Work of Wit
With the same Spirit that its Author *writ*,
Survey the *Whole*, nor seek slight Faults to find,
Where *Nature moves*, and *Rapture warms* the Mind;
Nor lose, for that malignant dull Delight,
The *gen'rous Pleasure* to be charm'd with Wit.
But in such Lays as neither *ebb*, nor *flow*,
Correctly cold, and *regularly low*,
That shunning Faults, one quiet *Tenour* keep;
We cannot *blame* indeed—but we may *sleep*.
In Wit, as Nature, what affects our Hearts
Is not th'Exactness of peculiar Parts;
'Tis not a *Lip*, or *Eye*, we Beauty call,
But the joint Force and full *Result* of *all*.

Thus when we view some well-proportion'd Dome,
(The *World*'s just Wonder, and ev'n *thine* O *Rome*!)
No single Parts unequally surprize;
All comes *united* to th' admiring Eyes;
No monstrous Height, or Breadth, or Length appear;
The *Whole* at once is *Bold*, and *Regular*.

    Whoever thinks a faultless Piece to see,
Thinks what ne'er was, nor is, nor e'er shall be.
In ev'ry Work regard the *Writer's End*,
Since none can compass more than they *Intend*;
And if the *Means* be just, the *Conduct* true,
Applause, in spite of trivial Faults, is due.
As Men of Breeding, sometimes Men of Wit,
T'avoid *great Errors*, must the *less* commit,
Neglect the Rules each *Verbal Critick* lays,
For *not* to know some Trifles, is a Praise.
Most Criticks, fond of some subservient Art,
Still make the *Whole* depend upon a *Part*,
They talk of *Principles*, but Notions prize,
And All to one lov'd Folly Sacrifice.

(lines 285–447)

Thus Criticks, of less *Judgment* than *Caprice*,
Curious, not *Knowing*, not *exact*, but *nice*,   calculating-
Form *short Ideas*; and offend in *Arts*
(As most in *Manners*) by a *Love to Parts*.

    Some to *Conceit* alone their Taste confine,
And glitt'ring Thoughts struck out at ev'ry Line;
Pleas'd with a Work where nothing's just or fit;
One *glaring Chaos* and *wild Heap* of *Wit*:
Poets like Painters, thus, unskill'd to trace
The *naked Nature* and the *living Grace*,
With *Gold* and *Jewels* cover ev'ry Part,
And hide with *Ornaments* their *Want of Art*.
True Wit is *Nature* to Advantage drest,

48

Def. of True Nature.

What oft was *Thought*, but ne'er so well *Exprest*,
Something, whose Truth convinc'd at Sight we find,
That gives us back the Image of our Mind:
As Shades more sweetly recommend the Light,
So modest Plainness sets off sprightly Wit:
For *Works* may have more *Wit* than does 'em good,
As *Bodies* perish through Excess of *Blood*.

   Others for *Language* all their Care express,
And value *Books*, as Women *Men*, for *Dress*:
Their Praise is still—*The Stile is excellent*:
The *Sense*, they humbly take upon Content.
Words are like *Leaves*; and where they most abound,
Much *Fruit* of *Sense* beneath is rarely found.
False Eloquence, like the *Prismatic Glass*,
Its gawdy Colours spreads on *ev'ry place*;
The Face of Nature we no more Survey,
All glares *alike*, without *Distinction* gay:
But true *Expression*, like th' unchanging *Sun*,
Clears, and *improves* whate'er it shines upon,
It *gilds* all Objects, but it *alters* none.
Expression is the *Dress* of *Thought*, and still
Appears more *decent* as more *suitable*;
A vile Conceit in pompous Words exprest,
Is like a Clown in regal Purple drest;
For diff'rent *Styles* with diff'rent *Subjects* sort, *suits*
As several Garbs with Country, Town, and Court.
Some by *Old Worlds* to Fame have made Pretence;
Ancients in *Phrase*, meer Moderns in their *Sense*!
Such *labour'd Nothings*, in so *strange* a Style,
Amaze th'unlearn'd, and make the Learned *Smiel*.
Unlucky, as *Fungoso* in the Play,
These Sparks with aukward Vanity display
What the Fine Gentleman wore *Yesterday*!
And but so mimick ancient Wits at best,
As Apes our Grandsires in their *Doublets drest*.

In *Words*, as *Fashions*, the same Rule will hold;
Alike Fantastick, if *too New*, or *Old*;
Be not the *first* by whom the *New* are try'd,
Nor yet the *last* to lay the *Old* aside.

metre .   But most by *Numbers* judge a Poet's Song,
And *smooth* or *rough*, with them, is *right* or *wrong*;
In the bright *Muse* tho' thousand *Charms* conspire,
Her *Voice* is all these tuneful Fools admire,
Who haunt *Parnassus* but to please their Ear,
Not mend their Minds; as some to *Church* repair,
Not for the *Doctrine*, but the *Musick* there.
These *Equal Syllables* alone require,
Tho' oft the Ear the *open Vowels* tire,
While *Expletives* their feeble Aid *do* join,
And ten low Words oft creep in one dull Line,
While they ring round the same *unvary'd Chimes*,
With sure *Returns* of still *expected Rhymes*.
Where-e'er you find *the cooling Western Breeze*,
In the next Line, it *whispers thro' the Trees*;
If *Chrystal Streams with pleasing Murmurs creep*,
The Reader's threaten'd (not in vain) with *Sleep*.
Then, at the *last*, and *only* Couplet fraught
With some *unmeaning* Thing they call a *Thought*,
A *needless Alexandrine* ends the Song,
That like a wounded Snake, drags its slow length
     along.
Leave such to tune their own dull Rhimes, and know
What's *roundly smooth*, or *languishingly slow*;
And praise the *Easie Vigor* of a Line,
Where *Denham*'s Strength, and *Waller*'s Sweetness
     join.
True Ease in Writing comes from Art, not Chance,
As those move easiest who have learn'd to dance.
'Tis not enough no Harshness gives Offence,
The *Sound* must seem an *Eccho* to the *Sense*.

Soft is the Strain when *Zephyr* gently blows,
And the *smooth Stream* in *smoother Numbers* flows;
But when loud Surges lash the sounding Shore,
The *hoarse, rough Verse* shou'd like the *Torrent* roar.
When *Ajax* strives, some Rocks' vast Weight to
  throw,
The Line too *labours*, and the Words move *slow*;
Not so, when swift *Camilla* scours the Plain,
Flies o'er th'unbending Corn, and skims along the
  Main.
Hear how *Timotheus*' vary'd Lays surprize,
And bid Alternate Passions fall and rise!
While, at each Change, the Son of *Lybian Jove*
Now *burns* with Glory, and then *melts* with Love;
Now his *fierce Eyes* with *sparkling Fury* glow;
Now *Sighs* steal out, and *Tears begin to flow*:
Persians and *Greeks* like *Turns of Nature* found,
And the *World's Victor* stood subdu'd by *Sound*!
The Pow'rs of Musick all our Hearts allow;
And what *Timotheus* was, is *Dryden* now.

  Avoid *Extreams*; and shun the Fault of such,
Who still are pleas'd *too little*, or *too much*.
At ev'ry Trifle scorn to take Offence,
That always shows *Great Pride*, or *Little Sense*;
Those *Heads* as *Stomachs* are not sure the best
Which nauseate all, and nothing can digest.
Yet let not each gay *Turn* thy Rapture move,
For Fools *Admire*, but Men of Sense *Approve*;
As things seem *large* which we thro' *Mists* descry,
Dulness is ever apt to *Magnify*.

  Some *foreign* Writers, some our *own* despise;
The *Ancients* only, or the *Moderns* prize:
(Thus *Wit*, like *Faith*, by each Man is apply'd
To *one small Sect*, and All are *damn'd beside*.)
Meanly they seek the Blessing to confine,

And force *that Sun* but on a *Part* to Shine;
Which not alone the *Southern Wit* sublimes,
But ripens Spirits in cold *Northern Climes*;
Which from the first has shone on *Ages past*,
Enlights the *present*, and shall warm the *last*:
(Tho' *each* may feel *Increases* and *Decays*,
And see now *clearer* and now *darker Days*)
Regard not then if Wit be *Old* or *New*,
But blame the *False*, and value still the *True*.

　　Some ne'er advance a Judgment of their own,
But *catch* the *spreading Notion* of the Town;
They reason and conclude by *Precedent*,
And own *stale Nonsense* which they ne'er invent.
Some judge of Authors' *Names*, not *Works*, and then
Nor praise nor blame the *Writings*, but the *Men*.
Of all this *Servile Herd* the worst is He
That in *proud Dulness* joins with *Quality*,
A constant Critick at the Great-man's Board,
To *fetch and carry* Nonsense for my Lord.
What *woful stuff* this Madrigal wou'd be,
In some starv'd Hackny Sonneteer, or me?
But let a *Lord* once own the *happy Lines*,
How the *Wit brightens*! How the *Style refines*!
Before *his* sacred Name flies ev'ry Fault,
And each *exalted* Stanza *teems* with *Thought*!

　　The *Vulgar* thus through *Imitation* err;
As oft the *Learn'd* by being *Singular*;
So much they scorn the Crowd, that if the Throng
By *Chance* go right, they *purposely* go wrong;
So Schismatics the *plain Believers* quit,
And are but damn'd for having *too much Wit*.

　　Some praise at Morning what they blame at Night;
— But always think the *last* Opinion *right*.
A Muse by these is like a Mistress us'd,
This hour she's *idoliz'd*, the next *abus'd*,

While their weak Heads, like Towns unfortify'd,
'Twixt Sense and Nonsense daily change their Side.
Ask them the Cause; *They're wiser still*, they say;
And still to Morrow's wiser than to Day.
We think our *Fathers* Fools, so *wise* we grow;
Our *wiser Sons*, no doubt, will think *us* so.
Once *School-Divines* this zealous Isle o'erspread;
Who knew most *Sentences* was *deepest read*;
Faith, Gospel, All, seem'd made to be *disputed*,
And none had *Sense enough to be Confuted*.
Scotists and *Thomists*, now, in Peace remain,
Amidst their *kindred Cobwebs* in *Duck-Lane*.
If *Faith* it self has *diff'rent Dresses* worn,
What wonder *Modes* in *Wit* shou'd take their Turn?

(*lines 560 to End*)

LEARN then what MORALS Criticks ought to show,
For 'tis but *half* a *Judge's Task*, to *Know*.
'Tis not enough, Taste, Judgment, Learning, join;
In all you speak, let Truth and Candor shine:
That not alone what to your *Sense* is due,
All may allow; but seek your *Friendship* too.

    Be *silent* always when you *doubt* your Sense;
And *speak*, tho' *sure*, with *seeming Diffidence*:
Some positive persisting Fops we know,
Who, if *once wrong*, will needs be *always so*;
But you, with Pleasure own your Errors past,
And make each Day a *Critick* on the last.

    'Tis not enough your Counsel still be *true*,
Blunt Truths more Mischief than *nice Falshoods* do;
Men must be *taught* as if you taught them *not*;
And Things *unknown* propos'd as Things *forgot*:
Without *Good Breeding*, *Truth* is disapprov'd;
That only makes *Superior* Sense *belov'd*.

    Be Niggards of Advice on no Pretence;

golden days of criticism

For the *worst Avarice* is that of *Sense*:
With mean Complacence ne'er betray your Trust,
Nor be so *Civil* as to prove *Unjust*;
Fear not the Anger of the Wise to raise;
Those best can *bear Reproof*, who *merit Praise*.
    'Twere well, might Criticks still this Freedom take;
But *Appius* reddens at each Word you speak,
And *stares*, *Tremendous*! with a *threatning Eye*,
Like some *fierce Tyrant* in *Old Tapestry*!
Fear most to tax an *Honourable* Fool,
Whose Right it is, *uncensur'd* to be dull;
Such without *Wit* are Poets when they please,
As without *Learning* they can take *Degrees*.
Leave dang'rous *Truths* to unsuccessful *Satyrs*,
And *Flattery* to fulsome *Dedicators*,
Whom, when they *Praise*, the World believes no more,
Than when they promise to give *Scribling* o'er.
'Tis best sometimes your Censure to restrain,
And *charitably* let the Dull be *vain*:
Your Silence there is better than your *Spite*,
For who can *rail* so long as they can *write*?
Still humming on, their drowzy Course they keep,
And *lash'd* so long, like *Tops*, are lash'd *asleep*.
False Steps but help them to renew the Race,
As after *Stumbling*, Jades will *mend* their Pace.
What Crouds of these, impenitently bold,
In *Sounds* and jingling *Syllables* grown old,
Still *run on* Poets in a raging Vein,
Ev'n to the Dregs and *Squeezings* of the *Brain*;
Strain out the last, dull droppings of their Sense,
And Rhyme with all the *Rage* of *Impotence*!
    Such shameless *Bards* we have; and yet 'tis true,
There are as mad, abandon'd *Criticks* too.

The Bookful Blockhead, ignorantly read,
With *Loads* of *Learned Lumber* in his Head,
With his own Tongue still edifies his Ears,
And always *List'ning to Himself* appears.
All Books he reads, and all he reads assails,
From *Dryden's Fables* down to *Durfey's Tales*.
With *him*, most Authors steal their Works, or buy;
Garth did not write his own *Dispensary*.
Name a new *Play*, and *he's* the Poet's *Friend*,
Nay show'd his Faults—but when wou'd Poets mend?
No Place so Sacred from such Fops is barr'd,
Nor is *Paul's Church* more safe than *Paul's Church-
      yard*:
Nay, fly to *Altars*; *there* they'll talk you dead;
For *Fools* rush in where *Angels* fear to tread.
Distrustful *Sense* with modest Caution speaks; ⎫
It still *looks home*, and *short Excursions* makes; ⎬
But *ratling Nonsense* in full *Vollies* breaks; ⎭
And never shock'd, and never turn'd aside,
Bursts out, resistless, with a thundring Tyde!
    But where's the Man, who Counsel *can* bestow,
Still *pleas'd to teach*, and yet not *proud to know*?
Unbiass'd, or by *Favour* or by *Spite*;
Not *dully prepossest*, nor *blindly right*;
Tho' Learn'd, well-bred; and tho' well-bred,
      sincere;
Modestly bold, and Humanly severe?
Who to a *Friend* his Faults can freely show,
And gladly praise the Merit of a *Foe*?
Blest with a *Taste* exact, yet unconfin'd;
A *Knowledge* both of *Books* and *Humankind*;
Gen'rous Converse; a *Soul* exempt from *Pride*;
And *Love to Praise*, with *Reason* on his Side?
    Such once were *Criticks*, such the Happy *Few*,
Athens and *Rome* in better Ages knew.

The mighty *Stagyrite* first left the Shore,
Spread all his Sails, and durst the Deeps explore;
He steer'd securely, and discover'd far,
Led by the Light of the *Mæonian Star*.
Poets, a *Race* long unconfin'd and free,
Still fond and proud of *Savage Liberty*,
Receiv'd his Laws, and stood convinc'd 'twas fit
Who conquer'd *Nature*, shou'd preside o'er *Wit*.

   Horace still charms with graceful Negligence,
And without Method *talks* us into Sense,
Will like a *Friend* familarly convey
The *truest Notions* in the *easiest way*.
He, who Supream in Judgment, as in Wit,
Might boldly censure, as he boldly writ,
Yet *judged* with *Coolness* tho' he sung with *Fire*;
His *Precepts* teach but what his *Works* inspire.
Our Criticks take a contrary Extream,
They *udge* with *Fury*, but they *write* with *Fle'me*:
Nor suffers *Horace* more in wrong *Translations*
By *Wits*, than *Criticks* in as wrong *Quotations*.

   See *Dionysius Homer*'s Thoughts refine,
And call new Beauties forth from ev'ry Line!

   Fancy and Art in gay *Petronius* please,
The *Scholar's Learning*, with the *Courtier's Ease*.

   In grave *Quintilian*'s copious Work we find
The justest *Rules*, and clearest *Method* join'd;
Thus *useful Arms* in Magazines we place,
All rang'd in *Order*, and dispos'd with *Grace*,
But less to please the Eye, than arm the Hand,
Still fit for Use, and ready at Command.

   Thee, bold *Longinus*! all the Nine inspire,
And bless *their Critick* with a *Poet's Fire*.
An ardent *Judge*, who Zealous in his Trust,
With *Warmth* gives Sentence, yet is always *Just*;
Whose *own Example* strengthens all his Laws,

And *Is himself* that great *Sublime* he draws.

Thus long succeeding Criticks justly reign'd,
Licence repress'd, and *useful Laws* ordain'd;
Learning and *Rome* alike in Empire grew,
And *Arts* still *follow'd* where her *Eagles flew*;
From the same Foes, at last, both felt their Doom,
And the same Age saw *Learning* fall, and *Rome*.
With *Tyranny*, then *Superstition* join'd.
As that the *Body*, this enslav'd the *Mind*;
Much was *Believ'd*, but little *understood*,
And to be *dull* was constru'd to be *good*;
A *second* Deluge Learning thus o'er-run,
And the *Monks* finish'd what the *Goths* begun.

At length, *Erasmus*, that *great*, *injur'd* Name,
(The *Glory* of the Priesthood, and the *Shame*!)
Stemm'd the *wild Torrent* of a *barb'rous Age*,
And drove those *Holy Vandals* off the Stage.

But see! each *Muse*, in *Leo's* Golden Days,
Starts from her Trance, and trims her wither'd Bays!
Rome's ancient *Genius*, o'er its *Ruins* spread,
Shakes off the *Dust*, and rears his rev'rend Head!
Then *Sculpture* and her *Sister-Arts* revive;
Stones leap'd to *Form*, and *Rocks* began to *live*;
With *sweeter Notes* each *rising Temple* rung;
A *Raphael* painted, and a *Vida* sung!
Immortal *Vida*! on whose honour'd Brow
The Poet's *Bays* and Critick's *Ivy* grow:
Cremona now shall ever boast thy Name,
As next in Place to *Mantua*, next in Fame!

But soon by Impious Arms from *Latium* chas'd,
Their *ancient Bounds* the banish'd Muses past;
Thence Arts o'er all the *Northern World* advance;
But *Critic Learning* flourish'd most in *France*.
The *Rules*, a Nation born to serve, obeys,
And *Boileau* still in Right of *Horace* sways.

But *we*, brave *Britons*, *Foreign Laws* despis'd,
And kept *unconquer'd*, and *unciviliz'd*,
Fierce for the *Liberties of Wit*, and bold,
We still defy'd the *Romans*, as *of old*.
Yet *some* there were, among the *sounder Few*
Of those who *less presum'd*, and *better knew*,
Who durst assert the *juster Ancient Cause*,
And here *restor'd* Wit's *Fundamental Laws*.
Such was the Muse, whose Rules and Practice tell,
Nature's chief Master-piece is writing well.
Such was *Roscomon*—not more *learn'd* than *good*,
With Manners gen'rous as his Noble Blood;
To him the Wit of *Greece* and *Rome* was known,
And ev'ry Author's *Merit*, but his own.
Such late was *Walsh*,—the Muse's Judge and Friend,
Who justly knew to blame or to commend;
To Failings *mild*, but *zealous* for Desert;
The *clearest Head*, and the *sincerest Heart*.
This humble Praise, lamented *Shade*! receive,
This Praise at least a grateful Muse may give!
The Muse, whose early Voice you taught to Sing,
Prescrib'd her Heights, and prun'd her tender Wing,
(Her Guide now lost) no more attempts to *rise*,
But in low Numbers short Excursions tries:
Content, if hence th' Unlearn'd their Wants may
      view,
The Learn'd reflect on what before they knew:
Careless of *Censure*, nor too fond of *Fame*,
Still pleas'd to *praise*, yet not afraid to *blame*,
Averse alike to *Flatter*, or *Offend*,
Not *free* from Faults, nor yet too vain to *mend*.

The Temple of Fame

This having heard and seen, some Pow'r unknown
Strait chang'd the Scene, and snatch'd me from the
    Throne.
Before my View appear'd a Structure fair,
Its Site uncertain, if in Earth or Air;
With rapid Motion turn'd the Mansion round;
With ceaseless Noise the ringing Walls resound:
Not less in Number were the spacious Doors,
Than Leaves on Trees, or Sands upon the Shores;
Which still unfolded stand, by Night, by Day,
Pervious to Winds, and open ev'ry way.
As Flames by Nature to the Skies ascend,
As weighty Bodies to the Center tend,
As to the Sea returning Rivers roll,
And the touch'd Needle trembles to the Pole:
Hither, as to their proper Place, arise
All various Sounds from Earth, and Seas, and Skies,
Or spoke aloud, or whisper'd in the Ear;
Nor ever Silence, Rest or Peace in here.
As on the smooth Expanse of Chrystal Lakes,
The sinking Stone at first a Circle makes;
The trembling Surface, by the Motion stir'd,
Spreads in a second Circle, then a third;
Wide, and more wide, the floating Rings advance,
Fill all the wat'ry Plain, and to the Margin dance.
Thus ev'ry Voice and Sound, when first they break,
On neighb'ring Air a soft Impression make;
Another ambient Circle then they move,
That, in its turn, impels the next above;

Thro undulating Air the Sounds are sent,
And spread o'er all the fluid Element.
  There various News I heard, of Love and Strife,
Of Peace and War, Health, Sickness, Death, and Life;
Of Loss and Gain, of Famine and of Store,
Of Storms at Sea, and Travels on the Shore,
Of Prodigies, and Portents seen in Air,
Of Fires and Plagues, and Stars with blazing Hair,
Of Turns of Fortune, Changes in the State,
The Falls of Fav'rites, Projects of the Great,
Of old Mismanagements, Taxations new—
All neither wholly false, nor wholly true.
  Above, below, without, within, around,
Confus'd, unnumber'd Multitudes are found,
Who pass, repass, advance, and glide away;
Hosts rais'd by Fear, and Phantoms of a Day.
Astrologers, that future Fates foreshew,
Projectors, Quacks, and Lawyers not a few;
And Priests and Party-Zealots, num'rous Bands
With home-born Lyes, or Tales from foreign Lands;
Each talk'd aloud, or in some secret Place,
And wild Impatience star'd in ev'ry Face:
The flying Rumours gather'd as they roll'd,
Scarce any Tale was sooner heard than told;
And all who told it, added something new, ⎫
And all who heard it, made Enlargements too, ⎬
In ev'ry Ear it spread, on ev'ry Tongue it grew. ⎭
Thus flying East and West, and North and South,
News travel'd with Increase from Mouth to Mouth;
So from a Spark that kindled first by Chance,
With gath'ring Force the quick'ning Flames advance;
Till to the Clouds their curling Heads aspire,
And Tow'rs and Temples sink in Floods of Fire.
  When thus ripe Lyes are to perfection sprung,
Full grown, and fit to grace a mortal Tongue,

Thro thousand Vents, impatient forth they flow,
And rush in Millions on the World below.
Fame sits aloft, and points them out their Course,
Their Date determines, and prescribes their Force:
Some to remain, and some to perish soon,
Or wane and wax alternate like the Moon.
Around, a thousand winged Wonders fly,
Born by the Trumpet's Blast, and scatter'd thro the Sky.

There, at one Passage, oft you might survey
A Lye and Truth contending for the way;
And long 'twas doubtful, both so closely pent,
Which first should issue thro the narrow Vent:
At last agreed, together out they fly,
Inseparable now, the Truth and Lye;
The strict Companions are for ever join'd,
And this or that unmix'd, no Mortal e'er shall find.

While thus I stood, intent to see and hear,
One came, methought, and whisper'd in my Ear;
What cou'd thus high thy rash Ambition raise?
Art thou, fond Youth, a Candidate for Praise?

'Tis true, said I, not void of Hopes I came,
For who so fond as youthful Bards of Fame?
But few, alas! the casual Blessing boast,
So hard to gain, so easy to be lost:
How vain that second Life in others' Breath,
Th' Estate which Wits inherit after Death!
Ease, Health, and Life, for this they must resign,
(Unsure the Tenure, but how vast the Fine!)
The Great Man's Curse,without the Gains endure,
Be envy'd, wretched, and be flatter'd, poor;
All luckless Wits their Enemies profest,
And all successful, jealous Friends at best.
Nor Fame I slight, nor for her Favours call;
She comes unlook'd for, if she comes at all:
But if the Purchase costs so dear a Price,

As soothing Folly, or exalting Vice:
Oh! if the Muse must flatter lawless Sway,
And follow still where Fortune leads the way;
Or if no Basis bear my rising Name,
But the fall'n Ruins of Another's Fame:
Then teach me, Heaven! to scorn the guilty Bays;
Drive from my Breast that wretched Lust of Praise;
Unblemish'd let me live, or die unknown,
Oh grant an honest Fame, or grant me none!

Windsor Forest

EXTRACTS

(lines 111–146)

See! from the Brake the whirring Pheasant springs,
And mounts exulting on triumphant Wings;
Short is his Joy! he feels the fiery Wound,
Flutters in Blood, and panting beats the Ground.
Ah!what avail his glossie, varying Dyes,
His Purple Crest, and Scarlet-circled Eyes,
The vivid Green his shining Plumes unfold;
His painted Wings, and Breast that flames with Gold?
Nor yet, when moist *Arcturus* clouds the Sky,
The Woods and Fields their pleasing Toils deny.
To Plains with well-breath'd Beagles we repair,
And trace the Mazes of the circling Hare.
(Beasts, urg'd by us, their Fellow Beasts pursue,
And learn of Man each other to undo.)
With slaught'ring Guns th'unweary'd Fowler roves,
When Frosts have whiten'd all the naked Groves;
Where Doves in Flocks the leafless Trees o'ershade,

And lonely Woodcocks haunt the watry Glade.
He lifts the Tube, and levels with his Eye;
Strait a short Thunder breaks the frozen Sky.
Oft, as in Airy Rings they skim the Heath,
The clam'rous Lapwings feel the Leaden Death:
Oft as the mounting Larks their Notes prepare,
They fall, and leave their little Lives in Air.

In genial Spring, beneath the quiv'ring Shade
Where cooling Vapours breathe along the Mead,
The patient Fisher takes his silent Stand
Intent, his Angle trembling in his Hand;
With Looks unmov'd, he hopes the Scaly Breed,
And eyes the dancing Cork and bending Reed.
Our plenteous Streams a various Race supply;
The bright-ey'd Perch with Fins of *Tyrian* Dye,
The silver Eel, in shining Volumes roll'd,
The yellow Carp, in Scales debrop'd with Gold,
Swift Trouts, diversify'd with Crimson Stains,
And Pykes, the Tyrants of the watry Plains.

(lines 329–422)

In That blest moment from his Oozy Bed
Old Father Thames advanc'd his rev'rend Head.
His Tresses dropt with Dews, and o'er the Stream
His shining Horns diffus'd a golden Gleam:
Grav'd on his Urn appear'd the Moon, that guides
His swelling Waters, and alternate Tydes;
The figur'd Streams in Waves of Silver roll'd,
And on their Banks *Augusta* rose in Gold.
Around his Throne the Sea-born Brothers stood,
Who swell with Tributary Urns his Flood.
First the fam'd Authors of his ancient Name,
The winding *Isis*, and the fruitful *Tame*:
The *Kennet* swift, for silver Eels renown'd;
The *Loddon* slow, with verdant Alders crown'd:

Cole, whose dark Streams his flow'ry Islands lave;
And chalky *Wey*, that rolls a milky Wave:
The blue, transparent *Vandalis* appears;
The gulphy *Lee* his sedgy Tresses rears:
And sullen *Mole*, that hides his diving Flood;
And silent *Darent*, stain'd with *Danish* Blood.

High in the midst, upon his Urn reclin'd,
(His Sea-green Mantle waving with the Wind)
The God appear'd; he turn'd his azure Eyes
Where *Windsor*-Domes and pompous Turrets rise,
Then bow'd and spoke; the Winds forget to roar,
And the hush'd Waves glide softly to the Shore.

Hail Sacred *Peace*! hail long-expected Days,
That *Thames's* Glory to the Stars shall raise!
Tho' *Tyber's* Streams immortal *Rome* behold,
Tho' foaming *Hermus* swells with Tydes of Gold,
From Heav'n it self tho' sev'nfold *Nilus* flows,
And Harvests on a hundred Realms bestows;
These now no more shall be the Muse's Themes,
Lost in my Fame, as in the Sea their Streams.
Let *Volga's* Banks with Iron Squadrons shine,
And Groves of Lances glitter on the *Rhine*,
Let barb'rous *Ganges* arm a servile Train;
Be mine the Blessings of a peaceful Reign.
No more my Sons shall dye with *British* Blood
Red *Iber's* Sands, or *Ister's* foaming Flood;
Safe on my Shore each unmolested Swain
Shall tend the Flocks, or reap the bearded Grain;
The shady Empire shall retain no Trace
Of War or Blood, but in the Sylvan Chace,
The Trumpets sleep, while chearful Horns are blown,
And Arms employ'd on Birds and Beasts alone.
Behold! th'ascending *Villa's* on my Side
Project long Shadows o'er the Chrystal Tyde.
Behold! *Augusta's* glitt'ring Spires increase,

And Temples rise, the beauteous Works of Peace.
I see, I see where two fair Cities bend
Their ample Bow, a new *White-Hall* ascend!
There mighty Nations shall inquire their Doom,
The World's great Oracle in Times to come;
There Kings shall sue, and suppliant States be seen
Once more to bend before a *British* QUEEN.

Thy Trees, fair *Windsor*! now shall leave their Woods,
And half thy Forests rush into my Floods,
Bear *Britain*'s Thunder, and her Cross display,
To the bright Regions of the rising Day;
Tempt Icy Seas, where scarce the Waters roll,
Where clearer Flames glow round the frozen Pole;
Or under Southern Skies exalt their Sails,
Led by new Stars, and born by spicy Gales!
For me the Balm shall bleed, and Amber flow,
The Coral redden, and the Ruby glow,
The Pearly Shell its lucid Globe infold,
And *Phoebus* warm the ripening Ore to Gold.
The Time shall come, when free as Seas or Wind
Unbounded *Thames* shall flow for all Mankind,
Whole Nations enter with each swelling Tyde,
And Seas but join the Regions they divide;
Earth's distant Ends our Glory shall behold,
And the new World launch forth to seek the Old.
Then Ships of uncouth Form shall stem the Tyde,
And Feather'd People crowd my wealthy Side,
And naked Youths and painted Chiefs admire
Our Speech, our Colour, and our strange Attire!
Oh stretch thy Rein, fair *Peace!* from Shore to Shore,
Till Conquest cease, and Slav'ry be no more:
Till the freed *Indians* in their native Groves
Reap their own Fruits, and woo their Sable Loves,
Peru once more a Race of Kings behold,
And other *Mexico*'s be roof'd with Gold.

E

Exil'd by Thee from Earth to deepest Hell,
In Brazen Bonds shall barb'rous *Discord* dwell:
Gigantick *Pride*, pale *Terror*, gloomy *Care*,
And mad *Ambition*, shall attend her there.
There purple *Vengeance* bath'd in Gore retires,
Her Weapons blunted, and extinct her Fires:
There hateful *Envy* her own Snakes shall feel,
And *Persecution* mourn her broken Wheel:
There *Faction* roar, *Rebellion* bite her Chain
And gasping Furies thirst for Blood in vain.

The Rape of the Lock

An Heroi-Comical Poem

Noleuram, Belinda, tuos violate capillos,
Sed juvat hoc precibus me tribuisse tuis.
MARTIAL

(*See the Introduction for an account of the action
of the first two Cantos*)

CANTO III

Close by those Meads for ever crown'd with Flow'rs,
Where *Thames* with Pride surveys his rising Tow'rs,
There stands a Structure of Majestick Frame,
Which from the neighb'ring *Hampton* takes its Name.
Here *Britain*'s Statesmen oft the Fall foredoom
Of Foreign Tyrants, and of Nymphs at home;
Here Thou, Great *Anna*! whom three Realms obey,
Dost sometimes Counsel take—and sometimes *Tea*.

Hither the Heroes and the Nymphs resort,
To taste awhile the Pleasures of a Court;
In various Talk th' instructive hours they past,

irony

Who gave the *Ball*, or paid the *Visit* last:
One speaks the Glory of the *British Queen*,
And one describes a charming *Indian Screen*;
A third interprets Motions, Looks, and Eyes;
At ev'ry Word a Reputation dies.
Snuff, or the *Fan*, supply each Pause of Chat,   *Irony*
With singing, laughing, ogling, and all that.

   Mean while declining from the Noon of Day,
The Sun obliquely shoots his burning Ray;
The hungry Judges soon the Sentence sign,
And Wretches hang that Jury-men may Dine;
The Merchant from th' *Exchange* returns in Peace,
And the long Labours of the *Toilette* cease—
Belinda now, whom Thirst of Fame invites,
Burns to encounter two adventrous Knights,
At <u>Ombre</u> singly to decide their Doom;
And swells her Breast with Conquests yet to come.
Strait the three Bands prepare in Arms to join,
Each Band the number of the Sacred Nine.
Soon as she spreads her Hand, th' Aerial Guard
Descend, and sit on each important Card:
First *Ariel* perch'd upon a *Matadore*,
Then each, according to the Rank they bore;
For *Sylphs*, yet mindful of their ancient Race,
Are, as when Women, wondrous fond of Place.

   Behold, four *Kings* in Majesty rever'd,
With hoary Whiskers and a forky Beard;
And four fair *Queens* whose hands sustain a Flow'r,
Th' expressive Emblem of their softer Pow'r;
Four *Knaves* in Garbs succinct, a trusty Band,
Caps on their heads, and Halberds in their hand;
And Particolour'd Troops, a shining Train,
Draw forth to Combat on the Velvet Plain.

   The skilful Nymph reviews her Force with Care;
Let Spades be Trumps! she said, and Trumps they were.

Now move to War her Sable *Matadores*,
In Show like Leaders of the swarthy *Moors*.
Spadillio first, unconquerable Lord!
Led off two captive Trumps, and swept the Board.
As many more *Manillio* forc'd to yield,
And march'd a Victor from the verdant Field.
Him *Basto* follow'd, but his Fate more hard
Gain'd but one Trump and one *Plebeian* Card.
With his broad Sabre next, a Chief in Years,
The hoary Majesty of *Spades* appears;
Puts forth one manly Leg, to sight reveal'd;
The rest his many-colour'd Robe conceal'd.
The Rebel-*Knave*, who dares his Prince engage,
Proves the just Victim of his Royal Rage.
Ev'n mighty *Pam* that Kings and Queen's o'erthrew,
And mow'd down Armies in the Fights of *Lu*,
Sad Chance of War! now, destitute of Aid,
Falls undistinguish'd by the Victor *Spade*!
  Thus far both Armies to *Belinda* yield;
Now to the *Baron* Fate inclines the Field.
His warlike *Amazon* her Host invades,
Th' Imperial Consort of the Crown of *Spades*.
The *Club*'s black Tyrant first her Victim dy'd,
Spite of his haughty Mien, and barb'rous Pride:
What boots the Regal Circle on his Head,
His Giant Limbs in State unwieldy spread?
That long behind he trails his pompous Robe,
And of all Monarchs only grasps the Globe?
  The *Baron* now his *Diamonds* pours apace;
Th' embroider'd *King* who shows but half his Face,
And his refulgent *Queen*, with Pow'rs combin'd,
Of broken Troops an easie Conquest find.
Clubs, *Diamonds*, *Hearts*, in wild Disorder seen,
With Throngs promiscuous strow the level Green.
Thus when dispers'd a routed Army runs,

Of *Asia*'s Troops, and *Africk*'s Sable Sons,
With like Confusion different Nations fly,
Of various Habit and of various Dye,
The pierc'd Battalions dis-united fall,
In Heaps on Heaps; one Fate o'erwhelms them all.

The *Knave of Diamonds* tries his wily Arts,
And wins (oh shameful Chance!) the *Queen of Hearts*.
At this, the Blood the Virgin's Cheek forsook,
A livid Paleness spreads o'er all her Look;
She sees, and trembles at th' approaching Ill,
Just in the Jaws of Ruin, and *Codille*.
And now, (as oft in some distemper'd State)
On one nice *Trick* depends the gen'ral Fate.
An *Ace* of Hearts steps forth: The *King* unseen
Lurk'd in her Hand, and mourn'd his captive *Queen*.
He springs to Vengeance with an eager pace,
And falls like Thunder on the prostrate *Ace*.
The Nymph exulting fills with Shouts the Sky,
The Walls, the Woods, and long Canals reply.

Oh thoughtless Mortals! ever blind to Fate,
Too soon dejected, and too soon elate!
Sudden these Honours shall be snatch'd away,
And curs'd for ever this Victorious Day.

For lo! the Board with Cups and Spoons is crown'd,
The Berries crackle, and the Mill turns round.
On shining Altars of *Japan* they raise
The silver Lamp; the fiery Spirits blaze.
From silver Spouts the grateful Liquors glide,
While <u>China</u>'s Earth receives the smoking Tyde.
At once they gratify their Scent and Taste,
And frequent Cups prolong the rich Repast.
Strait hover round the Fair her Airy Band;
Some, as she sip'd, the fuming Liquor fann'd,
Some o'er her Lap their careful Plumes display'd,
Trembling, and conscious of the rich Brocade.

69

Coffee, (which makes the Politician wise,
And see thro' all things with his half-shut Eyes)
Sent up in Vapours to the *Baron*'s Brain
New Stratagems, the radiant Lock to gain.
Ah cease rash Youth! desist ere 'tis too late,
Fear the just Gods, and think of *Scylla*'s Fate!
Chang'd to a Bird, and sent to flit in Air,
She dearly pays for *Nisus*' injur'd Hair!

　　But when to Mischief Mortals bend their Will,
How soon they find fit Instruments of Ill!
Just then, *Clarissa* drew with tempting Grace
Scissors — A two-edg'd Weapon from her shining Case,
So Ladies in Romance assist their Knight,
Present the Spear, and arm him for the Fight.
He takes the Gift with rev'rence, and extends
The little Engine on his Fingers' Ends,
This just behind *Belinda*'s Neck he spread,
As o'er the fragrant Steams she bends her Head:
Swift to the Lock a thousand Sprights repair,
A thousand Wings, by turns, blow back the Hair,
And thrice they twitch'd the Diamond in her Ear,
Thrice she look'd back, and thrice the Foe drew near.
Just in that instant, anxious *Ariel* sought
The close Recesses of the Virgin's Thought;
As on the Nosegay in her Breast reclin'd,
He watch'd th' Ideas rising in her Mind,
Sudden he view'd, in spite of all her Art,
An Earthly Lover lurking at her Heart.
Amaz'd, confus'd, he found his Pow'r expir'd,
Resign'd to Fate, and with a Sigh retir'd.

　　The Peer now spreads the glitt'ring *Forfex* wide, Scissors
T'inclose the Lock; now joins it, to divide.
Ev'n then, before the fatal Engine clos'd,
A wretched *Sylph* too fondly interpos'd;
Fate urg'd the Sheers, and cut the *Sylph* in twain,

(But Airy Substance soon unites again)
The meeting Points the sacred Hair dissever
From the fair Head, for ever and for ever!

Then flash'd the living Lightning from her Eyes,
And Screams of Horror rend th' affrighted Skies.
Not louder Shrieks to pitying Heav'n are cast,
When Husbands or when Lap-dogs breathe their last,
Or when rich *China* Vessels, fal'n from high,
In glittring Dust and painted Fragments lie!

Let Wreaths of Triumph now my Temples twine,
(The Victor cry'd) the glorious Prize is mine!
While Fish in Streams, or Birds delight in Air,
Or in a Coach and Six the *British* Fair,
As long as *Atalantis* shall be read,
Or the small Pillow grace a Lady's Bed,
While *Visits* shall be paid on solemn Days,
When numerous Wax-lights in bright Order blaze,
While Nymphs take Treats, or Assignations give,
So long my Honour, Name, and Praise shall live!

What Time wou'd spare, from Steel receives its date,
And Monuments, like Men, submit to Fate!
Steel cou'd the Labour of the Gods destroy,
And strike to Dust th' Imperial Tow'rs of *Troy*;
Steel cou'd the Works of mortal Pride confound,
And hew Triumphal Arches to the Ground.
What Wonder then, fair Nymph! thy Hairs shou'd feel
The conqu'ring Force of unresisted Steel?

CANTO IV

But anxious Cares the pensive Nymph opprest,
And secret Passions labour'd in her Breast.
Not youthful Kings in Battel seiz'd alive,
Not scornful Virgins who their Charms survive,
Not ardent Lovers robb'd of all their Bliss,

71

Not ancient Ladies when refus'd a Kiss,
Not Tyrants fierce that unrepenting die,
Not *Cynthia* when her *Manteau*'s pinn'd awry,
E'er felt such Rage, Resentment and Despair,
As Thou, sad Virgin! for thy ravish'd Hair.

For, that sad moment, when the *Sylphs* withdrew,
And *Ariel* weeping from *Belinda* flew,
Umbriel, a dusky melancholy Spright,
As ever sully'd the fair face of Light,
Down to the Central Earth, his proper Scene,
Repair'd to search the gloomy Cave of *Spleen*.

Swift on his sooty Pinions flitts the *Gnome*,
And in a Vapour reach'd the dismal Dome.
No cheerful Breeze this sullen Region knows,
The dreaded *East* is all the Wind that blows.
Here, in a Grotto, sheltred close from Air,
And screen'd in Shades from Day's detested Glare,
She sighs for ever on her pensive Bed,
Pain at her Side, and *Megrim* at her Head.

Two Handmaids wait the Throne: Alike in Place,
But diff'ring far in Figure and in Face.
Here stood *Ill-nature* like an *ancient Maid*,
Her wrinkled Form in *Black* and *White* array'd;
With store of Pray'rs, for Mornings, Nights, and Noons,
Her Hand is fill'd; her Bosom with Lampoons.

There *Affectation* with a sickly Mien
Shows in her Cheek the Roses of Eighteen,
Practis'd to Lisp, and hang the Head aside,
Faints into Airs, and languishes with Pride;
On the rich Quilt sinks with becoming Woe,
Wrapt in a Gown, for Sickness, and for Show.
The Fair-ones feel such Maladies as these,
When each new Night-Dress gives a new Disease.

A constant *Vapour* o'er the Palace flies;
Strange Phantoms rising as the Mists arise;

Dreadful, as Hermit's Dreams in haunted Shades,
Or bright as Visions of expiring Maids.
Now glaring Fiends, and Snakes on rolling Spires,
Pale Spectres, gaping Tombs, and Purple Fires:
Now Lakes of liquid Gold, *Elysian* Scenes,
And Crystal Domes, and Angels in Machines.

Unnumber'd Throngs on ev'ry side are seen
Of Bodies chang'd to various Forms by *Spleen*.
Here living *Teapots* stand, one Arm held out,
One bent; the Handle this, and that the Spout:
A Pipkin there like *Homer's Tripod* walks;
Here sighs a Jar, and there a Goose-pye talks;
Men prove with Child, as pow'rful Fancy works,
And Maids turn'd Bottels, call aloud for Corks.

Safe past the *Gnome* thro' this fantastick Band,
A Branch of healing *Spleenwort* in his hand. *plant - cures the splen*
Then thus addrest the Pow'r—Hail wayward Queen!
Who rule the Sex to Fifty from Fifteen,
Parent of Vapours and of Female Wit,
Who give th' *Hysteric* or *Poetic Fit*,
On various Tempers act by various ways,
Make some take Physick, others scribble Plays;
Who cause the Proud their Visits to delay,
And send the Godly in a Pett, to pray.
A Nymph there is, that all thy Pow'r disdains,
And thousands more in equal Mirth maintains.
But oh! if e'er thy *Gnome* could spoil a Grace,
Or raise a Pimple on a beauteous Face,
Like Citron-Waters Matrons' Cheeks inflame,
Or change Complexions at a losing Game;
If e'er with airy Horns I planted Heads,
Or rumpled Petticoats, or tumbled Beds,
Or caus'd Suspicion when no Soul was rude,
Or discompos'd the Head-dress of a Prude,
Or e'er to costive Lap-Dog gave Disease,

73

Which not the Tears of brightest Eyes could ease:
Hear me, and touch *Belinda* with Chagrin;
That single Act gives half the World the Spleen.
    The Goddess with a discontented Air
Seems to reject him, tho' she grants his Pray'r.
A wondrous Bag with both her Hands she binds,
Like that where once *Ulysses* held the Winds;
There she collects the Force of Female Lungs,
Sighs, Sobs, and Passions, and the War of Tongues.
A Vial next she fills with fainting Fears,
Soft Sorrows, melting Griefs, and flowing Tears.
The *Gnome* rejoicing bears her Gifts away,
Spreads his black Wings, and slowly mounts to Day.
    Sunk in *Thalestris*' Arms the Nymph he found,
Her Eyes dejected and her Hair unbound.
Full o'er their Heads the swelling Bag he rent,
And all the Furies issued at the Vent.
Belinda burns with more than mortal Ire,
And fierce *Thalestris* fans the rising Fire.
O wretched Maid! she spread her Hands, and cry'd,
(While *Hampton*'s Ecchos, wretched Maid! reply'd)
Was it for this you took such constant Care
The *Bodkin*, *Comb*, and *Essence* to prepare;
For this your Locks in Paper-Durance bound,
For this with tort'ring Irons wreath'd around?
For this with Fillets strain'd your tender Head,
And bravely bore the double Loads of Lead?
Gods! shall the Ravisher display your Hair,
While the Fops envy, and the Ladies stare!
Honour forbid! at whose unrival'd Shrine
Ease, Pleasure, Virtue, All, our Sex resign.
Methinks already I your Tears survey,
Already hear the horrid things they say,
Already see you a degraded Toast,
And all your Honour in a Whisper lost!

[margin annotation:] Connection with Prison

How shall I, then, your helpless Fame defend?
'Twill then be Infamy to seem your Friend!
And shall this Prize, th' inestimable Prize,
Expos'd thro' Crystal to the gazing Eyes,
And heighten'd by the Diamond's circling Rays,
On that Rapacious Hand for ever blaze?
Sooner shall Grass in *Hide*-Park *Circus* grow,
And Wits take Lodgings in the Sound of *Bow*;
Sooner let Earth, Air, Sea, to *Chaos* fall,
Men, Monkies, Lap-dogs, Parrots, perish all!

    She said, then raging to *Sir Plume* repairs,
And bids her *Beau* demand the precious Hairs:
(*Sir Plume*, of *Amber Snuff-box* justly vain,
And the nice Conduct of a *clouded Cane*)
With earnest Eyes, and round unthinking Face,
He first the Snuff-box open'd, then the Case,
And thus broke out—'My Lord, why, what the Devil?
Z—ds! damn the Lock! 'fore Gad, you must be civil!
Plague on't! 'tis past a Jest—nay prithee, Pox!
Give her the Hair!—he spoke, and rapp'd his Box.

    It grieves me much (reply'd the Peer again)
Who speaks so well shou'd ever speak in vain.
But by this Lock, this sacred Lock I swear,
(Which never more shall join its parted Hair,
Which never more its Honours shall renew,
Clipt from the lovely Head where late it grew)
That while my Nostrils draw the vital Air,
This Hand, which won it, shall for ever wear.
He spoke, and speaking, in proud Triumph spread
The long-contended Honours of her Head.

    But *Umbriel*, hateful *Gnome*! forbears not so;
He breaks the Vial whence the Sorrows flow.
Then see! the *Nymph* in beauteous Grief appears,
Her Eyes half-languishing, half-drown'd in Tears;
On her heav'd Bosom hung her drooping Head,

Which, with a Sigh, she rais'd; and thus she said.

　　For ever curs'd be this detested Day,
Which snatch'd my best, my fav'rite Curl away!
Happy! ah ten times happy, had I been,
If *Hampton-Court* these Eyes had never seen!
Yet am not I the first mistaken Maid,
By Love of *Courts* to num'rous Ills betray'd.
Oh had I rather un-admir'd remain'd
In some lone Isle, or distant *Northern* Land;
Where the gilt *Chariot* never marks the Way,
Where none learn *Ombre*, none e'er taste *Bohea*!
There kept my Charms conceal'd from mortal Eye,
Like Roses that in Desarts bloom and die.
What mov'd my Mind with youthful Lords to rome?
O had I stay'd, and said my Pray'rs at home!
'Twas this, the Morning *Omens* seem'd to tell;
Thrice from my trembling hand the *Patch-box* fell;
The tott'ring *China* shook without a Wind,
Nay, *Poll* sate mute, and *Shock* was most Unkind!
A *Sylph* too warn'd me of the Threats of Fate,
In mystic Visions, now believ'd too late!
See the poor Remnants of these slighted Hairs!
My hands shall rend what ev'n thy Rapine spares:
These, in two sable Ringlets taught to break,
Once gave new Beauties to the snowie Neck.
The Sister-Lock now sits uncouth, alone,
And in its Fellow's Fate foresees its own;
Uncurl'd it hangs, the fatal Sheers demands;
And tempts once more thy sacrilegious Hands.
Oh hadst thou, Cruel! been content to seize
Hairs less in sight, or any Hairs but these!

She said: the pitying Audience melt in Tears,
But *Fate* and *Jove* had stopp'd the *Baron's* Ears.
In vain *Thalestris* with Reproach assails,
For who can move when fair *Belinda* fails?
Not half so fixt the *Trojan* cou'd remain,
While *Anna* begg'd and *Dido* rag'd in vain.
Then grave *Clarissa* graceful wav'd her Fan;
Silence ensu'd, and thus the Nymph began.

Say, why are Beauties prais'd and honour'd most,
The wise Man's Passion, and the vain Man's Toast?
Why deck'd with all that Land and Sea afford,
Why Angels call'd, and Angel-like ador'd?
Why round our Coaches crowd the white-glov'd Beaus
Why bows the Side-box from its inmost Rows?
How vain are all these Glories, all our Pains,
Unless good Sense preserve what Beauty gains:
That Men may say, when we the Front-box grace,
Behold the first in Virtue, as in Face!
Oh! if to dance all Night, and dress all Day,
Charm'd the Small-pox, or chas'd old Age away;
Who would not scorn what Huswife's Cares produce,
Or who would learn one earthly Thing of Use?
To patch, nay ogle, might become a Saint,
Nor could it sure be such a Sin to paint.
But since, alas! frail Beauty must decay,
Curl'd or uncurl'd, since Locks will turn to grey,
Since painted, or not painted, all shall fade,
And she who scorns a Man, must die a Maid;
What then remains, but well our Pow'r to use,
And keep good Humour still whate'er we lose?
And trust me, Dear! good Humour can prevail,
When Airs, and Flights, and Screams, and Scolding fail.
Beauties in vain their pretty Eyes may roll;

Charms strike the Sight, but Merit wins the Soul.

So spoke the Dame, but no Applause ensu'd;
Belinda frown'd, *Thalestris* call'd her Prude.
To Arms, to Arms! the fierce Virago cries,
And swift as Lightning to the Combate flies.
All side in Parties, and begin th' Attack;
Fans clap, Silks russle, and tough Whalebones crack;
Heroes' and Heroins' Shouts confus'dly rise,
And base, and treble Voices strike the Skies.
No common Weapons in their Hands are found,
Like Gods they fight, nor dread a mortal Wound.

So when bold *Homer* makes the Gods engage,
And heav'nly Breasts with human Passions rage;
'Gainst *Pallas*, *Mars*; *Latona*, *Hermes* arms;
And all *Olympus* rings with loud Alarms.
Jove's Thunder roars, Heav'n trembles all around;
Blue *Neptune* storms, the bellowing Deeps resound;
Earth shakes her nodding Tow'rs, the Ground gives
      way;
And the pale Ghosts start at the Flash of Day!

Triumphant *Umbriel* on a Sconce's Height
Clapt his glad Wings, and sate to view the Fight:
Propt on their Bodkin Spears, the Sprights survey
The growing Combat, or assist the Fray.

While thro' the Press enrag'd *Thalestris* flies,
And scatters Deaths around from both her Eyes,
A *Beau* and *Witling* perish'd in the Throng,
One dy'd in *Metaphor*, and one in *Song*.
O cruel Nymph! a living Death I bear,
Cry'd *Dapperwit*, and sunk beside his Chair.
A mournful Glance Sir *Fopling* upwards cast,
Those Eyes are made so killing—was his last:
Thus on *Meander's* flow'ry Margin lies
Th' expiring Swan, and as he sings he dies.

When bold Sir *Plume* had drawn *Clarissa* down,

78

Chloe stept in, and kill'd him with a Frown;
She smil'd to see the doughty Hero slain,
But at her Smile, the Beau reviv'd again.

Now *Jove* suspends his golden Scales in Air,
Weighs the Men's Wits against the Lady's Hair;
The doubtful Beam long nods from side to side;
At length the Wits mount up, the Hairs subside.

See fierce *Belinda* on the *Baron* flies,
With more than usual Lightning in her Eyes;
Nor fear'd the Chief th' unequal Fight to try,
Who sought no more than on his Foe to die.
But this bold Lord, with manly Strength indu'd,
She with one Finger and a Thumb subdu'd:
Just where the Breath of Life his Nostrils drew,
A Charge of *Snuff* the wily Virgin threw;
The *Gnomes* direct, to ev'ry Atome just,
The pungent Grains of titillating Dust.
Sudden, with starting Tears each Eye o'erflows,
And the high Dome re-ecchoes to his Nose. *sneezes* .

Now meet thy Fate, incens'd *Belinda* cry'd,
And drew a deadly *Bodkin* from her Side.
(The same, his ancient Personage to deck,
Her great great Grandsire wore about his Neck
In three *Seal-Rings*; which after, melted down,
Form'd a vast *Buckle* for his Widow's Gown:
Her infant Grandame's *Whistle* next it grew,
The *Bells* she gingled, and the *Whistle* blew;
Then in a *Bodkin* grac'd her Mother's Hairs,
Which long she wore, and now *Belinda* wears.)

Boast not my Fall (he cry'd) insulting Foe!
Thou by some other shalt be laid as low.
Nor think, to die dejects my lofty Mind;
All that I dread, is leaving you behind!
Rather than so, ah let me still survive,
And burn in *Cupid's* Flames,—but burn alive.

Restore the lock! she cries; and all around
Restore the Lock! the vaulted Roofs rebound.
Not fierce *Othello* in so loud a Strain
Roar'd for the Handkerchief that caus'd his Pain.
But see how oft Ambitious Aims are cross'd,
And Chiefs contend 'till all the Prize is lost!
The Lock, obtain'd with Guilt, and kept with Pain,
In ev'ry place is sought, but sought in vain:
With such a Prize no Mortal must be blest,
So Heav'n decrees! with Heav'n who can contest?
 Some thought it mounted to the Lunar Sphere,
Since all things lost on Earth, are treasur'd there.
There Heroes' Wits are kept in pondrous Vases,
And Beaus in *Snuff-boxes* and *Tweezer-Cases*.
There broken Vows, and Death-bed Alms are found,
And Lovers' Hearts with Ends of Riband bound;
The Courtier's Promises, and Sick Man's Pray'rs,
The Smiles of Harlots, and the Tears of Heirs,
Cages for Gnats, and Chains to Yoak a Flea;
Dry'd Butterflies, and Tomes of Casuistry.
 But trust the Muse—she saw it upward rise,
Tho' mark'd by none but quick Poetic Eyes:
(So *Rome*'s great Founder to the Heav'ns withdrew,
To *Proculus* alone confess'd in view.)
A sudden Star, it shot thro' liquid Air,
And drew behind a radiant *Trail of Hair*.
Not *Berenice*'s Locks first rose so bright,
The Heav'ns bespangling with dishevel'd Light.
The *Sylphs* behold it kindling as it flies,
And pleas'd pursue its Progress thro' the Skies.
 This the *Beau-monde* shall from the *Mall* survey,
And hail with Musick its propitious Ray.
This, the blest Lover shall for *Venus* take,
And send up Vows from *Rosamonda*'s Lake.
This *Partridge* soon shall view in cloudless Skies,

When next he looks thro' *Galilaeo*'s Eyes;
And hence th' Egregious Wizard shall foredoom
The Fate of *Louis*, and the Fall of *Rome*.
   Then cease, bright Nymph! to mourn thy ravish'd
      Hair
Which adds new Glory to the shining Sphere!
Not all the Tresses that fair Head can boast
Shall draw such Envy as the Lock you lost.
For, after all the Murders of your Eye,
When, after Millions slain, your self shall die;
When those fair Suns shall sett, as sett they must,
And all those Tresses shall be laid in Dust;
This Lock, the Muse shall consecrate to Fame,
And mid'st the Stars inscribe *Belinda*'s Name!

A Farewell to London. In the Year 1715

    Dear, damn'd, distracting Town, farewell!
      Thy Fools no more I'll teize:
    This Year in Peace, ye Critics, dwell,
        Ye Harlots, sleep at Ease!

    Soft *Bethel* and rough *Craggs*, adieu!
        Earl *Warwick* make your Moan,
    The lively *Hinchinbrook* and you
        May knock up Whores alone.

    To drink and droll be *Rowe* allow'd
        Till the third watchman toll;
    Let *Jervase* gratis paint, and *Frowd*
        Save Three-pence, and his Soul.

Farewell *Arbuthnot*'s Raillery
    On every learned Sot;
And *Garth*, the best good Christian he,
    Altho' he knows it not.

Lintot, farewell! thy Bard must go;
    Farewell, unhappy *Tonson*!
Heaven gives thee for thy Loss of *Rowe*,
    Lean *Philips*, and fat *Johnson*.

Why should I stay? Both Parties rage;
    My vixen Mistress squalls;
The Wits in envious Feuds engage;
    And *Homer* (damn him!) calls.

The Love of Arts lies cold and dead
    In *Hallifax*'s Urn;
And not one Muse of all he fed,
    Has yet the Grace to mourn.

M Friends, by Turns, my Friends confound,
    Betray, and are betray'd:
Poor *Younger*'s sold for Fifty Pound,
    And *Bicknell* is a Jade.

Why make I Friendships with the Great,
    When I no Favour seek?
Or follow Girls Seven Hours in Eight?—
    I need but once a Week.

Still idle, with a busy Air,
    Deep Whimsies to contrive;
The gayest Valetudinaire,
    Most thinking Rake alive.

Solicitous for others Ends,
    Tho' fond of dear Repose;
Careless or drowsy with my Friends,
    And frolick with my Foes.

Laborious Lobster-nights, farewell!
    For sober, studious Days;
And *Burlington*'s delicious Meal,
    For Sallads, Tarts, and Pease!

Adieu to all but *Gay* alone,
    Whose Soul, sincere and free,
Loves all Mankind, but flatters none,
    And so may starve with me.

Ode on Solitude

Happy the man, whose wish and care
A few paternal acres bound,
Content to breathe his native air,
                In his own ground.

Whose herds with milk, whose fields with bread,
Whose flocks supply him with attire,
Whose trees in summer yield him shade,
                In winter fire.

Blest! who can unconcern'dly find
Hours, days, and years slide soft away,
In health of body, peace of mind,
                Quiet by day,

Sound sleep by night; study and ease
Together mix'd; sweet recreation,
And innocence, which most does please,
        With meditation.

Thus let me live, unseen, unknown;
Thus unlamented let me dye;
Steal from the world, and not a stone
        Tell where I lye.

Pope stated that this poem was 'written at about twelve years old';
but the earliest extant draft dates from 1709.

Verses Occasion'd by an &c. at the End of Mr. D'Urfy's Name in the Title to one of his Plays

Jove call'd before him t'other Day
The *Vowels, U, O, I, E, A,*
All *Dipthongs*, and all *Consonants*,
Either of *England* or of *France*;
And all that were, or wish'd to be,
Rank'd in the Name of *Tom D'Urfy*.

Fierce in this Cause, the *Letters* spoke all,
Liquids grew rough, and *Mutes* turn'd vocal:
Those four proud Syllables alone
Were silent, which by Fates Decree
Chim'd in so smoothly, one by one,
To the sweet Name of *Tom D'Urfy*.

N, by whom Names subsist, declar'd,
To have no Place in this was hard:
And *Q* maintain'd 'twas but his Due
Still to keep Company with *U*;
So hop'd to stand no less than he
In the great Name of *Tom D'Urfy*.

E shew'd, a *Comma* ne'er could claim
A Place in any *British* Name;
Yet making here a perfect Botch,
Thrusts your poor Vowell from his Notch:
Hiatus mi valde deflendus!
From which good *Jupiter* defend us!
Sooner I'd quit my Part in thee,
Than be no Part in *Tom D'Urfy*.

P protested, puff'd, and swore,
He'd not be serv'd so like a Beast;
He was a Piece of Emperor,
And made up half a Pope at least.
C vow'd, he'd frankly have releas'd
His double Share in *Caesar Caius*,
For only one in *Tom Durfeius*.

I, Consonant and Vowel too,
To *Jupiter* did humbly sue,
That of his Grace he would proclaim
Durfeius his true *Latin* Name;
For tho' without them both, 'twas clear,
Himself could ne'er be *Jupiter*;
Yet they'd resign that Post so high,
To be the Genetive, *Durfei*.

B and *L* swore Bl— and W—s
X and *Z* cry'd, P—x and Z—s
G swore, by G—d, it ne'er should be;
And *W* would not lose, not he,
An *English Letter*'s Property,
In the great Name of *Tom Durfy*.

In short, the rest were all in Fray,
From *Christcross* to *Et caetera*.
They, tho' but Standers-by too, mutter'd;
Dipthongs, and Tripthongs, swore and stutter'd,
That none had so much Right to be ⎫
Part of the Name of stuttering *T*— ⎬
T—*Tom*—*a*—*as*—*De*—*Dur*—*fe*—*fy*. ⎭

Then *Jove* thus spake: With Care and Pain
We form'd this Name, renown'd in Rhyme;
Not thine, Immortal *Neufgermain*!
Cost studious *Cabalists* more Time.
Yet now, as then, you all declare, ⎫
Far hence to *Egypt* you'll repair, ⎬
And turn strange Hieroglyphicks there; ⎭
Rather than Letters longer be,
Unless i' th' Name of *Tom D'Urfy*.

Were you all pleas'd, yet what I pray,
To foreign Letters cou'd I say?
What if the *Hebrew* next should aim
To turn quite backward *D'Urfy*'s Name?
Should the *Greek* quarrel too, by *Styx*, I
Cou'd ne'er bring in *Psi* and *Xi*;
Omicron and *Omega* from us
Wou'd each hope to be *O* in *Thomas*;
And all th' ambitious Vowels vie, ⎫
No less than *Pythagorick Y*, ⎬
To have a Place in *Tom D'Urfy*. ⎭

Then, well-belov'd and trusty Letters!
Cons'nants! and Vowels, (much their betters,)
We, willing to repair this Breach,
And, all that in us lies, please each;
Et caet'ra to our Aid must call,
Et caet'ra represents ye all:
Et caet'ra therefore, we decree,
Henceforth for ever join'd shall be
To the great Name of *Tom Durfy*.

To Mr. John Moore, Author of the Celebrated Worm-Powder

How much, egregious *Moor*, are we
   Deceiv'd by Shews and Forms!
Whate'er we think, whate'er we see,
   All Humankind are Worms.

Man is a very Worm by Birth,
   Vile Reptile, weak, and vain!
A while he crawls upon the Earth,
   Then shrinks to Earth again.

That Woman is a Worm we find,
   E'er since our Grandame's Evil;
She first convers'd with her own Kind,
   That antient Worm, the Devil.

The Learn'd themselves we Book-Worms name;
   The Blockhead is a Slow-worm;
The Nymph whose Tail is all on Flame
   Is aptly term'd a Glow-worm:

The Fops are painted Butterflies,
　　That flutter for a Day;
First from a Worm they take their Rise,
　　And in a Worm decay:

The Flatterer an Earwig grows;
　　Thus Worms suit all Conditions;
Misers are Muckworms, Silk-worms Beaus,
　　And Death-watches Physicians.

That Statesmen have the Worm, is seen
　　By all their winding Play;
Their Conscience is a Worm within,
　　That gnaws them Night and Day.

Ah *Moore!* thy Skill were well employ'd,
　　And greater Gain would rise,
If thou could'st make the Courtier void
　　The Worm that never dies!

O learned Friend of *Abchurch-Lane,*
　　Who sett'st our Entrails free!
Vain is thy Art, thy Powder vain,
　　Since Worms shall eat ev'n thee.

Our Fate thou only can'st adjourn
　　Some few short Years, no more!
Ev'n *Button's* Wits to Worms shall turn,
　　Who Maggots were before.

Three Epitaphs on
John Hewet and Sarah Drew

I

When Eastern lovers feed the fun'ral fire,
On the same pile the faithful fair expire;
Here pitying heav'n that virtue mutual found,
And blasted both, that it might neither wound.
Hearts so sincere th' Almighty saw well pleas'd,
Sent his own lightning, and the Victims seiz'd.

II. EPITAPH ON JOHN HEWET AND SARAH DREW
IN THE CHURCHYARD AT STANTON HARCOURT

NEAR THIS PLACE LIE THE BODIES OF
JOHN HEWET AND SARAH DREW
AN INDUSTRIOUS YOUNG MAN, AND
VIRTUOUS MAIDEN OF THIS PARISH;
CONTRACTED IN MARRIAGE
WHO BEING WITH MANY OTHERS AT HARVEST
WORK, WERE BOTH IN AN INSTANT KILLED
BY LIGHTNING ON THE LAST DAY OF JULY
1718

Think not by rigorous judgment seiz'd,
    A pair so faithful could expire;
Victims so pure Heav'n saw well pleas'd
    And snatch'd them in Cœlestial fire.

Live well and fear no sudden fate;
    When God calls Virtue to the grave,
Alike tis Justice, soon or late,
    Mercy alike to kill or save.

Virtue unmov'd can hear the Call,
And face the Flash that melts the Ball.

Here lye two poor Lovers, who had the mishap
Tho very chaste people, to die of a Clap.

The Lamentation of Glumdalclitch, for the Loss of Grildrig. A Pastoral

Soon as *Glumdalclitch* mist her pleasing Care,
She wept, she blubber'd, and she tore her Hair.
No *British* Miss sincerer Grief has known,
Her Squirrel missing, or her Sparrow flown.
She furl'd her Sampler, and hawl'd in her Thread,
And stuck her Needle into *Grildrig*'s Bed:
Then spread her Hands, and with a Bounce let fall
Her Baby, like the Giant in *Guild-hall*.
In Peals of Thunder now she roars, and now
She gently whimpers like a lowing Cow.
Yet lovely in her Sorrow still appears:
Her Locks dishevell'd, and her Flood of Tears
Seem like the lofty Barn of some rich Swain,
When from the Thatch drips fast a Show'r of Rain.

In vain she search'd each Cranny of the House,
Each gaping Chink impervious to a Mouse.
'Was it for this (she cry'd) with daily Care
Within thy Reach I set the Vinegar?
And fill'd the Cruet with the Acid Tide,
While Pepper-Water-Worms thy Bait supply'd;

Where twin'd the Silver Eel around thy Hook,
And all the little Monsters of the Brook.
Sure in that Lake he dropt—My *Grilly*'s drown'd'—
She dragg'd the Cruet, but no *Grildrig* found.

'Vain is thy Courage, *Grilly*, vain thy Boast;
But little Creatures enterprise the most.
Trembling, I've seen thee dare the Kitten's Paw;
Nay, mix with Children, as they play'd at Taw;
Nor fear the Marbles, as they bounding flew:
Marbles to them, but rolling Rocks to you.

'Why did I trust thee with that giddy Youth?
Who from a *Page* can ever learn the Truth?
Vers'd in Court Tricks, that Money-loving Boy
To some Lord's Daughter sold the living Toy;
Or rent him Limb from Limb in cruel Play,
As Children tear the Wings of Flies away;
From Place to Place o'er *Brobdingnag* I'll roam,
And never will return, or bring thee home.
But who hath Eyes to trace the passing Wind,
How then thy fairy Footsteps can I find?
Dost thou bewilder'd wander all alone,
In the green Thicket of a Mossy Stone,
Or tumbled from the Toadstool's slipp'ry Round,
Perhaps all maim'd, lie grov'ling on the Ground?
Dost thou, inbosom'd in the lovely Rose,
Or sunk within the Peach's Down, repose?

Within the King-Cup if thy Limbs are spread,
Or in the golden Cowslip's Velvet Head;
O show me, *Flora*, 'midst those Sweets, the Flow'r
Where sleeps my *Grildrig* in his fragrant Bow'r!
'But ah! I fear thy little Fancy roves
On little Females, and on little Loves;
Thy Pigmy Children, and thy tiny Spouse,

The Baby Play-things that adorn thy House,
Doors, Windows, Chimnies, and the spacious Rooms,
Equal in Size to Cells of Honeycombs.
Hast thou for these now ventur'd from the Shore,
Thy Bark a Bean-shell, and a Straw thy Oar?
Or in thy Box, now bounding on the Main?
Shall I ne'er bear thy self and House again?
And shall I set thee on my Hand no more,
To see thee leap the Lines, and traverse o'er
My spacious Palm? Of Stature scarce a Span,
Mimick the Actions of a real Man?
No more behold thee turn my Watches Key,
As Seamen at a Capstern Anchors weigh?
How wert thou wont to walk with cautious Tread,
A Dish of Tea like Milk-Pail on thy Head?
How chase the Mite that bore thy Cheese away,
And keep the rolling Maggot at a Bay?'

She said, but broken Accents stopt her Voice,
Soft as the Speaking Trumpet's mellow Noise:
She sobb'd a Storm, and wip'd her flowing Eyes,
Which seem'd like two broad Suns in misty Skies:
O squander not thy Grief, those Tears command
To weep upon our Cod in *Newfound-land*:
The plenteous Pickle shall preserve the Fish,
And *Europe* taste thy Sorrows in a Dish.

The Words of the King of Brobdingnag, as he held Captain Gulliver between his Finger and Thumb for the Inspection of the Sages and Learned Men of the Court

In Miniature see *Nature*'s Power appear;
Which wings the Sun-born Insects of the Air,
Which frames the Harvest-bug, too small for Sight,
And forms the Bones and Muscles of the Mite!
Here view him stretch'd. The Microscope explains,
That the Blood, circling, flows in human Veins;
See, in the Tube he pants, and sprawling lies,
Stretches his little Hands, and rolls his Eyes!

Smit with his Countrey's Love, I've heard him prate
Of Laws and Manners in his Pigmy State.
By travel, generous Souls enlarge the Mind,
Which home-bred Prepossession had confin'd;
Yet will he boast of many Regions known,
But still, with partial Love, extol his own.
He talks of Senates, and of Courtly Tribes,
Admires their Ardour, but forgets their Bribes;
Of hireling Lawyers tells the just Decrees,
Applauds their Eloquence, but sinks their Fees.
Yet who his Countrey's partial Love can blame?
'Tis sure some Virtue to conceal its Shame.

The World's the native City of the Wise;
He sees his *Britain* with a Mother's Eyes;
Softens Defects, and heightens all its Charms,
Calls it the Seat of Empire, Arts and Arms!
Fond of his Hillock Isle, his narrow Mind
Thinks Worth, Wit, Learning, to that Spot confin'd;

Thus Ants, who for a Grain employ their Cares,
Think all the Business of the Earth is theirs.
Thus Honey-combs seem Palaces to Bees;
And Mites imagine all the World a Cheese.

When Pride in such contemptuous Beings lies,
In Beetles, Britons, Bugs and Butterflies,
Shall we, like Reptiles, glory in Conceit?
Humility's the Virtue of the Great.

An Essay on Man

Moral.

or the First Book of Ethic Epistles to
H. St. John L. Bolingbroke

THE SECOND EPISTLE

Know then thyself, presume not God to scan;
The proper study of Mankind is Man.
Plac'd on this isthmus of a middle state,
A being darkly wise, and rudely great:
With too much knowledge for the Sceptic side,
With too much weakness for the Stoic's pride,
He hangs between; in doubt to act, or rest
In doubt to deem himself a God, or Beast;
In doubt his Mind or Body to prefer,
Born but to die, and reas'ning but to err;
Alike in ignorance, his reason such,
Whether he thinks too little, or too much:
Chaos of Thought and Passion, all confus'd;
Still by himself abus'd, or disabus'd;
Created half to rise, and half to fall;
Great lord of all things, yet a prey to all;

94

Sole judge of Truth, in endless Error hurl'd:
The glory, jest, and riddle of the world!
   Go, wond'rous creature! mount where Science
     guides,
Go, measure earth, weigh air, and state the tides;
Instruct the planets in what orbs to run,
Correct old Time, and regulate the Sun;
Go, soar with Plato to th' empyreal sphere,
To the first good, first perfect, and first fair;
Or tread the mazy round his follow'rs trod,
And quitting sense call imitating God;
As Eastern priests in giddy circles run,
And turn their heads to imitate the Sun.
Go, teach Eternal Wisdom how to rule—
Then drop into thyself, and be a fool!
   Superior beings, when of late they saw
A mortal Man unfold all Nature's law,
Admir'd such wisdom in an earthly shape,
And shew'd a NEWTON as we shew an Ape.
   Could he, whose rules the rapid Comet bind,
Describe or fix one movement of his Mind?
Who saw its fires here rise, and there descend,
Explain his own beginning, or his end?
Alas what wonder! Man's superior part
Uncheck'd may rise, and climb from art to art:
But when his own great work is but begun,
What Reason weaves, by Passion is undone.
   Trace Science then, with Modesty thy guide;
First strip off all her equipage of Pride,
Deduct what is but Vanity, or Dress,
Or Learning's Luxury, or Idleness;
Or tricks to shew the stretch of human brain,
Mere curious pleasure, or ingenious pain:
Expunge the whole, or lop th' excrescent parts
Of all, our Vices have created Arts:

Then see how little the remaining sum,
Which serv'd the past, and must the times to come!
  II. Two Principles in human nature reign;
Self-love, to urge, and Reason, to restrain;
Nor this a good, nor that a bad we call,
Each works its end, to move or govern all:
And to their proper operation still,
Ascribe all Good; to their improper, Ill.

  Self-love, the spring of motion, acts the soul;
Reason's comparing balance rules the whole.
Man, but for that, no action could attend,
And, but for this, were active to no end;
Fix'd like a plant on his peculiar spot,
To draw nutrition, propagate, and rot;
Or, meteor-like, flame lawless thro' the void,
Destroying others, by himself destroy'd.

  Most strength the moving principle requires;
Active its task, it prompts, impels, inspires.
Sedate and quiet the comparing lies,
Form'd but to check, delib'rate, and advise.
Self-love still stronger, as its objects nigh;
Reason's at distance, and in prospect lie:
That sees immediate good by present sense;
Reason, the future and the consequence.
Thicker than arguments, temptations throng,
At best more watchful this, but that more strong.
The action of the stronger to suspend
Reason still use, to Reason still attend:
Attention, habit and experience gains,
Each strengthens Reason, and Self-love restrains.

  Let subtle schoolmen teach these friends to fight,
More studious to divide than to unite,
And Grace and Virtue, Sense and Reason split,
With all the rash dexterity of Wit:
Wits, just like fools, at war about a Name,

Have full as oft no meaning, or the same.
Self-love and Reason to one end aspire,
Pain their aversion, Pleasure their desire;
But greedy that its object would devour,
This taste the honey, and not wound the flow'r:
Pleasure, or wrong or rightly understood,
Our greatest evil, or our greatest good.
   III. Modes of Self-love the Passions we may call;
'Tis real good, or seeming, moves them all;
But since not every good we can divide,
And Reason bids us for our own provide;
Passions, tho' selfish, if their means be fair,
List under Reason, and deserve her care;
Those, that imparted, court a nobler aim,
Exalt their kind, and take some Virtue's name.

   In lazy Apathy let Stoics boast
Their Virtue fix'd; 'tis fix'd as in a frost,
Contracted all, retiring to the breast;
But strength of mind is Exercise, not Rest:
The rising tempest puts in act the soul,
Parts it may ravage, but preserves the whole.
On life's vast ocean diversely we sail,
Reason the card, but Passion is the gale;
Nor God alone in the still calm we find,
He mounts the storm, and walks upon the wind.

   Passions, like Elements, tho' born to fight,
Yet, mix'd and soften'd, in his work unite:
These 'tis enough to temper and employ;
But what composes Man, can Man destroy?
Suffice that Reason keep to Nature's road,
Subject, compound them, follow her and God.
Love, Hope, and Joy, fair pleasure's smiling train,
Hate, Fear, and Grief, the family of pain;
These mix'd with art, and to due bounds confin'd,
Make and maintain the balance of the mind:

G

The lights and shades, whose well accorded strife
Gives all the strength and colour of our life.

Pleasures are ever in our hands or eyes,
And when in act they cease, in prospect rise;
Present to grasp, and future still to find,
The whole employ of body and of mind.
All spread their charms, but charm not all alike;
On diff'rent senses diff'rent objects strike;
Hence diff'rent Passions more or less inflame,
As strong or weak, the organs of the frame;
And hence one master Passion in the breast,
Like Aaron's serpent, swallows up the rest.

As Man, perhaps, the moment of his breath,
Receives the lurking principle of death;
The young disease, that must subdue at length,
Grows with his growth, and strengthens with his
strength
So, cast and mingled with his very frame,
The Mind's disease, its ruling Passion came;
Each vital humour which should feed the whole,
Soon flows to this, in body and in soul.
Whatever warms the heart, or fills the head,
As the mind opens, and its functions spread,
Imagination plies her dang'rous art,
And pours it all upon the peccant part.

Nature its mother, Habit is its nurse;
Wit, Spirit, Faculties, but make it worse;
Reason itself but gives it edge and pow'r;
As Heaven's blest beam turns vinegar more sowr;
We, wretched subjects tho' to lawful sway,
In this weak queen, some fav'rite still obey.
Ah! if she lend not arms, as well as rules,
What can she more than tell us we are fools?
Teach us to mourn our Nature, not to mend,
A sharp accuser, but a helpless friend!

Or from a judge turn pleader, to persuade
The choice we make, or justify it made;
Proud of an easy conquest all along,
She but removes weak passions for the strong:
So, when small humors gather to a gout,
The doctor fancies he has driv'n them out.

    Yes, Nature's road must ever be prefer'd;
Reason is here no guide, but still a guard:
'Tis hers to rectify, not overthrow,
And treat this passion more as friend than foe:
A mightier Pow'r the strong direction sends,
And sev'ral Men impels to sev'ral ends.
Like varying winds, by other passions tost,
This drives them constant to a certain coast.
Let pow'r or knowledge, gold or glory, please,
Or (oft more strong than all) the love of ease;
Thro' life 'tis followed, ev'n at life's expence;
The merchant's toil, the sage's indolence,
The monk's humility, the hero's pride,
All, all alike, find Reason on their side.

    Th' Eternal Art educing good from ill,
Grafts on this Passion our best principle:
'Tis thus the Mercury of Man is fix'd,
Strong grows the Virtue with his nature mix'd;
The dross cements what else were too refin'd,
And in one interest body acts with mind.

    As fruits ungrateful to the planter's care
On savage stocks inserted learn to bear;
The surest Virtues thus from Passions shoot,
Wild Nature's vigor working at the root.
What crops of wit and honesty appear
From spleen, from obstinacy, hate, or fear!
See anger, zeal and fortitude supply;
Ev'n av'rice, prudence; sloth, philosophy;
Lust, thro' some certain strainers well refin'd,

Is gentle love, and charms all womankind:
Envy, to which th' ignoble mind's a slave,
Is emulation in the learn'd or brave:
Nor Virtue, male or female, can we name,
But what will grow on Pride, or grow on Shame.

Thus Nature gives us (let it check our pride)
The virtue nearest to our vice ally'd;
Reason the byass turns to good from ill,
And Nero reigns a Titus, if he will.
The fiery soul abhor'd in Catiline,
In Decius charms, in Curtius is divine.
The same ambition can destroy or save,
And make a patriot as it makes a knave.

IV. This light and darkness in our chaos join'd,
What shall divide? The God within the mind.

Extremes in Nature equal ends produce,
In Man they join to some mysterious use;
Tho' each by turns the other's bound invade,
As, in some well-wrought picture, light and shade,
And oft so mix, the diff'rence is too nice
Where ends the Virtue, or begins the Vice.

Fools! who from hence into the notion fall,
That Vice or Virtue there is none at all.
If white and black blend, soften, and unite
A thousand ways, is there no black or white?
Ask your own heart, and nothing is so plain;
'Tis to mistake them, costs the time and pain.

V. Vice is a monster of so frightful mien,
As, to be hated, needs but to be seen;
Yet seen too oft, familiar with her face,
We first endure, then pity, then embrace.
But where th' Extreme of Vice, was ne'er agreed:
Ask where's the North? at York, 'tis on the Tweed;
In Scotland, at the Orcades; and there,
At Greenland, Zembla, or the Lord knows where:

No creature owns it in the first degree,
But thinks his neighbour farther gone than he.
Ev'n those who dwell beneath its very zone,
Or never feel the rage, or never own;
What happier natures shrink at with affright,
The hard inhabitant contends is right.

VI. Virtuous and vicious ev'ry Man must be,
Few in th' extreme, but all in the degree;
The rogue and fool by fits is fair and wise,
And ev'n the best, by fits, what they despise.
'Tis but by parts we follow good or ill,
For, Vice or Virtue, Self directs it still;
Each individual seeks a sev'ral goal;
But HEAV'N's great view is One, and that the Whole:
That counter-works each folly and caprice;
That disappoints th' effect of ev'ry vice:
That happy frailties to all ranks apply'd,
Shame to the virgin, to the matron pride,
Fear to the statesman, rashness to the chief,
To kings presumption, and to crowds belief,
That Virtue's ends from Vanity can raise,
Which seeks no int'rest, no reward but praise;
And build on wants, and on defects of mind,
The joy, the peace, the glory of Mankind.

Heav'n forming each on other to depend,
A master, or a servant, or a friend,
Bids each on other for assistance call,
'Till one Man's weakness grows the strength of all.
Wants, frailties, passions closer still ally
The common int'rest, or endear the tie:
To these we owe true friendship, love sincere,
Each home-felt joy that life inherits here:
Yet from the same we learn, in its decline,
Those joys, those loves, those int'rests to resign:
Taught half by Reason, half by mere decay,

To welcome death, and calmly pass away.
   Whate'er the Passion, knowledge, fame, or pelf,
Not one will change his neighbor with himself.
The learn'd is happy nature to explore,
The fool is happy that he knows no more;
The rich is happy in the plenty giv'n,
The poor contents him with the care of Heav'n.
See the blind beggar dance, the cripple sing.
The sot a hero, lunatic a king;
The starving chemist in his golden views
Supremely blest, the poet in his muse.
   See some strange comfort ev'ry state attend,
And Pride bestow'd on all, a common friend;
See some fit Passion ev'ry age supply,
Hope travels thro', nor quits us when we die.
   Behold the child, by Nature's kindly law,
Pleas'd with a rattle, tickled with a straw:
Some livelier play-thing gives his youth delight,
A little louder, but as empty quite:
Scarfs, garters, gold, amuse his riper stage;
And beads and pray'r-books are the toys of age:
Pleas'd with this bauble still, as that before;
'Till tir'd he sleeps, and Life's poor play is o'er!
   Mean-while Opinion gilds with varying rays
Those painted clouds that beautify our days;
Each want of happiness by Hope supply'd,
And each vacuity of sense by Pride:
These build as fast as knowledge can destroy;
In Folly's cup still laughs the bubble, joy;
One prospect lost, another still we gain;
And not a vanity is giv'n in vain;
Ev'n mean Self-love becomes, by force divine,
The scale to measure others wants by thine.
See! and confess, one comfort still must rise,
'Tis this, Tho' Man's a fool, yet GOD IS WISE.

Moral Essays

Epistle II. To a Lady

OF THE CHARACTERS OF WOMEN

ARGUMENT

Of the Characters of *Women* (consider'd only as contra-
distinguished from the other Sex). That these are yet
more inconsistent and incomprehensible than those of
Men, of which Instances are given even from such
Characters as are plainest, and most strongly mark'd;
as in the *Affected*, Ver. 7, &c. The *Soft-natur'd*. 29. the
Cunning, 45. the *Whimsical*, 53. the *Wits and Refiners*,
87. the *Stupid* and *Silly*, 101. How Contrarieties run
thro' them all.

But tho' the *Particular Characters* of this Sex are
more various than those of Men, the *General Charac-
teristick*, as to the *Ruling Passion*, is more uniform and
confin'd. In what That lies, and whence it *proceeds*, 207,
&c. Men are best known in publick Life, Women in
private, 199. What are the *Aims*, and the *Fate* of the
Sex, both as to *Power* and *Pleasure*? 219, 231, &c.
Advice for their true Interest, 249. The Picture of an
esteemable Woman, made up of the best kind of
Contrarieties, 269, &c.

Nothing so true as what you once let fall,
'Most Women have no Characters at all'.
Matter too soft a lasting mark to bear,
And best distinguish'd by black, brown, or fair.
    How many pictures of one Nymph we view,
All how unlike each other, all how true!
Arcadia's Countess, here, in ermin'd pride,
Is there, Pastora by a fountain side:

Here Fannia, leering on her own good man,
Is there, a naked Leda with a Swan.
Let then the Fair one beautifully cry,
In Magdalen's loose hair and lifted eye,
Or drest in smiles of sweet Cecilia shine,
With simp'ring Angels, Palms, and Harps divine;
Whether the Charmer sinner it, or saint it,
If Folly grows romantic, I must paint it.

Come then, the colours and the ground prepare!
Dip in the Rainbow, trick her off in Air,
Chuse a firm Cloud, before it fall, and in it
Catch, ere she change, the Cynthia of this minute.

Rufa, whose eye quick-glancing o'er the Park,
Attracts each light gay meteor of a Spark,
Agrees as ill with Rufa studying Locke,
As Sappho's diamonds with her dirty smock,
Or Sappho at her toilet's greasy task,
With Sappho fragrant at an ev'ning Mask:
So morning Insects that in muck begun,
Shine, buzz, and fly-blow in the setting-sun.

How soft is Silia! fearful to offend,
The Frail one's advocate, the Weak one's friend:
To her, Calista prov'd her conduct nice,
And good Simplicius asks of her advice.
Sudden, she storms! she raves! You tip the wink,
But spare your censure; Silia does not drink.
All eyes may see from what the change arose,
All eyes may see—a Pimple on her nose.

Papillia, wedded to her doating spark,
Sighs for the shades—'How charming is a Park!'
A Park is purchas'd, but the Fair he sees
All bath'd in tears—'Oh odious, odious Trees!'

Ladies, like variegated Tulips, show,
'Tis to their Changes that their charms we owe;
Their happy Spots the nice admirer take,

Fine by defect, and delicately weak.
'Twas thus Calypso once each heart alarm'd,
Aw'd without Virtue, without Beauty charm'd;
Her Tongue bewitch'd as odly as her Eyes,
Less Wit than Mimic, more a Wit than wise:
Strange graces still, and stranger flights she had,
Was just not ugly, and was just not mad;
Yet ne'er so sure our passion to create,
As when she touch'd the brink of all we hate.

    Narcissa's nature, tolerably mild,
To make a wash, would hardly stew a child,
Has ev'n been prov'd to grant a Lover's pray'r,
And paid a Tradesman once to make him stare,
Gave alms at Easter, in a Christian trim,
And made a Widow happy, for a whim.
Why then declare Good-nature is her scorn,
When 'tis by that alone she can be born?
Why pique all mortals, yet affect a name?
A fool to Pleasure, and a slave to Fame:
Now deep in Taylor and the Book of Martyrs,
Now drinking citron with his Grace and Chartres.
Now Conscience chills her, and now Passion burns;
And Atheism and Religion take their turns;
A very Heathen in the carnal part,
Yet still a sad, good Christian at her heart.

    See Sin in State, majestically drunk,
Proud as a Peeress, prouder as a Punk;
Chaste to her Husband, frank to all beside,
A teeming Mistress, but a barren Bride.
What then? let Blood and Body bear the fault,
Her Head's untouch'd, that noble Seat of Thought:
Such this day's doctrine—in another fit
She sins with Poets thro' pure Love of Wit.
What has not fir'd her bosom or her brain?
Cæsar and Tall-boy, Charles and Charlema'ne.

As Helluo, late Dictator of the Feast,
The Nose of Hautgout, and the Tip of Taste,
Critick'd your wine, and analyz'd your meat,
Yet on plain Pudding deign'd at-home to eat;
So Philomedé, lect'ring all mankind
On the soft Passion, and the Taste refin'd,
Th' Address, the Delicacy—stoops at once,
And makes her hearty meal upon a Dunce.

Flavia's a Wit, has too much sense to Pray,
To Toast our wants and wishes, is her way;
Nor asks of God, but of her Stars to give
The mighty blessing, 'while we live, to live.'
Then all for Death, that Opiate of the soul!
Lucretia's dagger, Rosamonda's bowl.
Say, what can cause such impotence of mind?
A Spark too fickle, or a Spouse too kind.
Wise Wretch! with Pleasures too refin'd to please,
With too much Spirit to be e'er at ease,
With too much Quickness ever to be taught,
With too much Thinking to have common Thought:
Who purchase Pain with all that Joy can give,
And die of nothing but a Rage to live.

Turn then from Wits; and look on Simo's Mate,
No Ass so meek, no Ass so obstinate:
Or her, that owns her Faults, but never mends,
Because she's honest, and the best of Friends:
Or her, whose life the Church and Scandal share,
For ever in a Passion, or a Pray'r:
Or her, who laughs at Hell, but (like her Grace)
Cries, 'Ah! how charming if there's no such place!'
Or who in sweet vicissitude appears
Of Mirth and Opium, Ratafie and Tears,
The daily Anodyne, and nightly Draught,
To kill those foes to Fair ones, Time and Thought.
Woman and Fool are two hard things to hit,

For true No-meaning puzzles more than Wit.
  But what are these to great Atossa's mind?
Scarce once herself, by turns all Womankind!
Who, with herself, or others, from her birth
Finds all her life one warfare upon earth:
Shines, in exposing Knaves, and painting Fools,
Yet is, whate'er she hates and ridicules.
No Thought advances, but her Eddy Brain
Whisks it about, and down it goes again.
Full sixty years the World has been her Trade,
The wisest Fool much Time has ever made.
From loveless youth to unrespected age,
No Passion gratify'd except her Rage.
So much the Fury still out-ran the Wit,
The Pleasure miss'd her, and the Scandal hit.
Who breaks with her, provokes Revenge from Hell,
But he's a bolder man who dares be well:
Her ev'ry turn with Violence pursu'd,
Nor more a storm her Hate than Gratitude.
To that each Passion turns, or soon or late;
Love, if it makes her yield, must make her hate:
Superiors? death! and Equals? what a curse!
But an Inferior not dependant? worse.
Offend her, and she knows not to forgive;
Oblige her, and she'll hate you while you live:
But die, and she'll adore you—Then the Bust
And Temple rise—then fall again to dust.
Last night, her Lord was all that's good and great,
A Knave this morning, and his Will a Cheat.
Strange! by the Means defeated of the Ends,
By Spirit robb'd of Pow'r, by Warmth of Friends,
By Wealth of Follow'rs! without one distress
Sick of herself thro' very selfishness!
Atossa, curs'd with ev'ry granted pray'r,
Childless with all her Children, wants an Heir.

To Heirs unknown descends th' unguarded store
Or wanders, Heav'n directed, to the Poor.
  Pictures like these, dear Madam, to design,
Asks no firm hand, and no unerring line;
Some wand'ring touch, or some reflected light,
Some flying stroke alone can hit 'em right:
For how should equal Colours do the knack?
Chameleons who can paint in white and black?
  'Yet Cloe sure was form'd without a spot—'
Nature in her then err'd not, but forgot.
'With ev'ry pleasing, ev'ry prudent part,
Say, what can Cloe want?'—she wants a Heart.
She speaks, behaves, and acts just as she ought;
But never, never, reach'd one gen'rous Thought.
Virtue she finds too painful an endeavour,
Content to dwell in Decencies for ever.
So very reasonable, so unmov'd,
As never yet to love, or to be lov'd.
She, while her Lover pants upon her breast,
Can mark the figures on an Indian chest;
And when she sees her Friend in deep despair,
Observes how much a Chintz exceeds Mohair.
Forbid it Heav'n, a Favour or a Debt
She e'er should cancel—but she may forget.
Safe is your Secret still in Cloe's ear;
But none of Cloe's shall you ever hear.
Of all her Dears she never slander'd one,
But cares not if a thousand are undone.
Would Cloe know if you're alive or dead?
She bids her Footman put it in her head.
Cloe is prudent—would you too be wise?
Then never break your heart when Cloe dies.
  One certain Portrait may (I grant) be seen,
Which Heav'n has varnish'd out, and made a *Queen*:
The same for ever! and describ'd by all

With Truth and Goodness, as with Crown and Ball:
Poets heap Virtues, Painters Gems at will,
And show their zeal, and hide their want of skill.
'Tis well—but, Artists! who can paint or write,
To draw the Naked is your true delight:
That Robe of Quality so struts and swells,
None see what Parts of Nature it conceals.
Th' exactest traits of Body or of Mind,
We owe to models of an humble kind.
If QUEENSBERRY to strip there's no compelling,
'Tis from a Handmaid we must take a Helen.
From Peer or Bishop 'tis no easy thing
To draw the man who loves his God, or King:
Alas! I copy (or my draught would fail)
From honest Mah'met, or plain Parson Hale.

But grant, in Public Men sometimes are shown,
A Woman's seen in Private life alone:
Our bolder Talents in full light display'd,
Your Virtues open fairest in the shade.
Bred to disguise, in Public 'tis you hide;
There, none distinguish 'twixt your Shame or Pride,
Weakness or Delicacy; all so nice,
That each may seem a Virtue, or a Vice.

In Men, we various Ruling Passions find,
In Women, two almost divide the kind;
Those, only fix'd, they first or last obey,
The Love of Pleasure, and the Love of Sway.

That, Nature gives; and where the lesson taught
Is but to please, can Pleasure seem a fault?
Experience, this; by Man's oppression curst,
They seek the second not to lose the first.

Men, some to Bus'ness, some to Pleasure take;
But ev'ry Woman is at heart a Rake:
Men, some to Quiet, some to public Strife;
But ev'ry Lady would be Queen for life.

Yet mark the fate of a whole Sex of Queens!
Pow'r all their end, but Beauty all the means.
In Youth they conquer, with so wild a rage,
As leaves them scarce a Subject in their Age:
For foreign glory, foreign joy, they roam;
No thought of Peace or Happiness at home.
But Wisdom's Triumph is well-tim'd Retreat,
As hard a science to the Fair as Great!
Beauties, like Tyrants, old and friendless grown,
Yet hate to rest, and dread to be alone,
Worn out in public, weary ev'ry eye,
Nor leave one sigh behind them when they die.

Pleasures the sex, as children Birds, pursue,
Still out of reach, yet never out of view,
Sure, if they catch, to spoil the Toy at most,
To covet flying, and regret when lost:
At last, to follies Youth could scarce defend,
'Tis half their Age's prudence to pretend;
Asham'd to own they gave delight before,
Reduc'd to feign it, when they give no more:
As Hags hold Sabbaths, less for joy than spight,
So these their merry, miserable Night;
Still round and round the Ghosts of Beauty glide,
And haunt the places where their Honour dy'd.

See how the World its Veterans rewards!
A Youth of frolicks, an old Age of Cards,
Fair to no purpose, artful to no end,
Young without Lovers, old without a Friend,
A Fop their Passion, but their Prize a Sot,
Alive, ridiculous, and dead, forgot!

Ah Friend! to dazzle let the Vain design,
To raise the Thought and touch the Heart, be thine!
That Charm shall grow, while what fatigues the Ring
Flaunts and goes down, an unregarded thing.
So when the Sun's broad beam has tir'd the sight,

All mild ascends the Moon's more sober light,
Serene in Virgin Modesty she shines,
And unobserv'd the glaring Orb declines.

Oh! blest with Temper, whose unclouded ray
Can make to morrow chearful as to day;
She, who can love a Sister's charms, or hear
Sighs for a Daughter with unwounded ear;
She, who ne'er answers till a Husband cools,
Or, if she rules him, never shows she rules;
Charms by accepting, by submitting sways,
Yet has her humour most, when she obeys;
Lets Fops or Fortune fly which way they will;
Disdains all loss of Tickets, or Codille;
Spleen, Vapours, or Small-pox, above them all,
And Mistress of herself, tho' China fall.

And yet, believe me, good as well as ill,
Woman's at best a Contradiction still.
Heav'n, when it strives to polish all it can
Its last best work, but forms a softer Man;
Picks from each sex, to make its Fav'rite blest,
Your love of Pleasure, our desire of Rest,
Blends, in exception to all gen'ral rules,
Your Taste of Follies, with our Scorn of Fools,
Reserve with Frankness, Art with Truth ally'd,
Courage with Softness, Modesty with Pride,
Fix'd Principles, with Fancy ever new;
Shakes all together, and produces—You.

Be this a Woman's Fame: with this unblest,
Toasts live a scorn, and Queens may die a jest.
This Phœbus promis'd (I forget the year)
When those blue eyes first open'd on the sphere;
Ascendant Phœbus watch'd that hour with care,
Averted half your Parents simple Pray'r,
And gave you Beauty, but deny'd the Pelf
Which buys your sex a Tyrant o'er itself.

The gen'rous God, who Wit and Gold refines,
And ripens Spirits as he ripens Mines,
Kept Dross for Duchesses, the world shall know it,
To you gave Sense, Good-humour, and a Poet.

Epistle III. To Allen Lord Bathurst

EXTRACT

(lines 21–248)

What Nature wants, commodious Gold bestows,
'Tis thus we eat the bread another sows:
But how unequal it bestows, observe,
'Tis thus we riot, while who sow it, starve.
What Nature wants (a phrase I much distrust)
Extends to Luxury, extends to Lust:
And if we count among the Needs of life
Another's Toil, why not another's Wife?
Useful, I grant, it serves what life requires,
But dreadful too, the dark Assassin hires:
Trade it may help, Society extend;
But lures the Pyrate, and corrupts the Friend:
It raises Armies in a Nation's aid,
But bribes a Senate, and the Land's betray'd.
    Oh! that such bulky Bribes as all might see,
Still, as of old, incumber'd Villainy!
In vain may Heroes fight, and Patriots rave;
If secret Gold saps on from knave to knave.
Could France or Rome divert our brave designs,
With all their brandies or with all their wines?
What could they more than Knights and Squires con-
        found,

Or water all the Quorum ten miles round?
A Statesman's slumbers how this speech would spoil!
'Sir, Spain has sent a thousand jars of oil;
Huge bales of British cloth blockade the door;
A hundred oxen at your levee roar.'

Poor Avarice one torment more would find;
Nor could Profusion squander all in kind.
Astride his cheese Sir Morgan might we meet,
And Worldly crying coals from street to street,
(Whom with a wig so wild, and mien so maz'd,
Pity mistakes for some poor tradesman craz'd).
Had Colepepper's whole wealth been hops and hogs,
Could he himself have sent it to the dogs?
His Grace will game: to White's a Bull be led,
With spurning heels and with a butting head.
To White's be carried, as to ancient games,
Fair Coursers, Vases, and alluring Dames.
Shall then Uxorio, if the stakes he sweep,
Bear home six Whores, and make his Lady weep?
Or soft Adonis, so perfum'd and fine,
Drive to St. James's a whole herd of swine?
Oh filthy check on all industrious skill,
To spoil the nation's last great trade, Quadrille!

Once, we confess, beneath the Patriot's cloak,
From the crack'd bag the dropping Guinea spoke,
And gingling down the back-stairs, told the crew,
'Old Cato is as great a Rogue as you.'
Blest paper-credit! last and best supply!
That lends Corruption lighter wings to fly!
Gold imp'd by thee, can compass hardest things,
Can pocket States, can fetch or carry Kings;
A single leaf shall waft an Army o'er,
Or ship off Senates to a distant Shore;
A leaf, like Sibyl's, scatter to and fro
Our fates and fortunes, as the winds shall blow:

Pregnant with thousands flits the Scrap unseen,
And silent sells a King, or buys a Queen.
　Since then, my Lord, on such a World we fall,
What say you? 'Say? Why take it, Gold and all.'
　What Riches give us let us then enquire:
Meat, Fire, and Cloaths. What more? Meat, Cloaths,
　　and Fire.
Is this too little? would you more than live?
Alas! 'tis more than Turner finds they give.
Alas! 'tis more than (all his Visions past)
Unhappy Wharton, waking, found at last!
What can they give? to dying Hopkins Heirs;
To Chartres, Vigour; Japhet, Nose and Ears?
Can they, in gems bid pallid Hippia glow,
In Fulvia's buckle ease the throbs below,
Or heal, old Narses, thy obscener ail,
With all th' embroid'ry plaister'd at thy tail?
They might (were Harpax not too wise to spend)
Give Harpax self the blessing of a Friend;
Or find some Doctor that would save the life
Of wretched Shylock, spite of Shylock's Wife:
But thousands die, without or this or that,
Die, and endow a College, or a Cat:
To some, indeed, Heav'n grants the happier fate,
T'enrich a Bastard, or a Son they hate.
　Perhaps you think the Poor might have their part?
Bond damns the Poor, and hates them from his heart:
The grave Sir Gilbert holds it for a rule,
That 'every man in want is knave or fool:'
'God cannot love (says Blunt, with tearless eyes)
The wretch he starves'—and piously denies:
But the good Bishop, with a meeker air,
Admits　and leaves them Providence's care.
　Yet, to be just to these poor men of pelf,
Each does but hate his Neighbour as himself:

Damn'd to the Mines, an equal fate betides
The Slave that digs it, and the Slave that hides.
Who suffer thus, mere Charity should own,
Must act on motives pow'rful, tho' unknown:
Some War, some Plague, or Famine they foresee,
Some Revelation hid from you and me.
Why Shylock wants a meal, the cause is found,
He thinks a Loaf will rise to fifty pound.
What made Directors cheat in South-sea year?
To live on Ven'son when it sold so dear.
Ask you why Phryne the whole Auction buys?
Phryne foresees a general Excise.
Why she and Sappho raise that monstrous sum?
Alas! they fear a man will cost a plum.

Wise Peter sees the World's respect for Gold,
And therefore hopes this Nation may be sold:
Glorious Ambition! Peter, swell thy store,
And be what Rome's great Didius was before.

The Crown of Poland, venal twice an age,
To just three millions stinted modest Gage.
But nobler scenes Maria's dreams unfold,
Hereditary Realms, and worlds of Gold.
Congenial souls! whose life one Av'rice joins,
And one fate buries in th' Asturian Mines.

Much injur'd Blunt! why bears he Britain's hate?
A wizard told him in these words our fate:
'At length Corruption, like a gen'ral flood,
(So long by watchful Ministers withstood)
Shall deluge all; and Av'rice creeping on,
Spread like a low-born mist, and blot the Sun;
Statesman and Patriot ply alike the stocks,
Peeress and Butler share alike the Box,
And Judges job, and Bishops bite the town,
And mighty Dukes pack cards for half a crown.
See Britain sunk in lucre's sordid charms,

And France reveng'd of ANNE's and EDWARD's arms!'
No mean Court-badge, great Scriv'ner! fir'd thy brain,
Nor lordly Luxury, nor City Gain:
No, 'twas thy righteous end, asham'd to see
Senates degen'rate, Patriots disagree,
And nobly wishing Party-rage to cease,
To buy both sides, and give thy Country peace.

   'All this is madness,' cries a sober sage:
But who, my friend, has reason in his rage?

   'The ruling Passion, be it what it will,
The ruling Passion conquers Reason still.'
Less mad the wildest whimsey we can frame,
Than ev'n that Passion, if it has no Aim;
For tho' such motives Folly you may call,
The Folly's greater to have none at all.

   Hear then the truth: ' 'Tis Heav'n each Passion
      sends,
And diff'rent men directs to diff'rent ends.
Extremes in Nature equal good produce,
Extremes in Man concur to gen'ral use.'
Ask we what makes one keep, and one bestow?
That POW'R who bids the Ocean ebb and flow,
Bids seed-time, harvest, equal course maintain,
Thro' reconcil'd extremes of drought and rain,
Builds Life on Death, on Change Duration founds,
And gives th'eternal wheels to know their rounds.

   Riches, like insects, when conceal'd they lie,
Wait but for wings, and in their season, fly.
Who sees pale Mammon pine amidst his store,
Sees but a backward steward for the Poor;
This year a Reservoir, to keep and spare,
The next a Fountain, spouting thro' his Heir,
In lavish streams to quench a Country's thirst,
And men and dogs shall drink him 'till they burst.

   Old Cotta sham'd his fortune and his birth,

Yet was not Cotta void of wit or worth:
What tho' (the use of barb'rous spits forgot)
His kitchen vy'd in coolness with his grot?
His court with nettles, moats with cresses stor'd,
With soups unbought and sallads blest his board.
If Cotta liv'd on pulse, it was no more
Than Bramins, Saints, and Sages did before;
To cram the Rich was prodigal expence,
And who would take the Poor from Providence?
Like some lone Chartreux stands the good old Hall,
Silence without, and Fasts within the wall;
No rafter'd roofs with dance and tabor sound,
No noontide-bell invites the country round;
Tenants with sighs the smoakless tow'rs survey,
And turn th' unwilling steeds another way:
Benighted wanderers, the forest o'er,
Curse the sav'd candle, and unop'ning door;
While the gaunt mastiff growling at the gate,
Affrights the beggar whom he longs to eat.
   Not so his Son, he mark'd this oversight,
And then mistook reverse of wrong for right.
(For what to shun will no great knowledge need,
But what to follow, is a task indeed.)
What slaughter'd hecatombs, what floods of wine,
Fill the capacious Squire, and deep Divine!
Yet no mean motive this profusion draws,
His oxen perish in his country's cause;
'Tis GEORGE and LIBERTY that crowns the cup,
And Zeal for that great House which eats him up.
The woods recede around the naked seat,
The Sylvans groan—no matter—for the Fleet:
Next goes his Wool—to clothe our valiant bands,
Last, for his Country's love, he sells his Lands.
To town he comes, completes the nation's hope,
And heads the bold Train-bands, and burns a Pope.

And shall not Britain now reward his toils,
Britain, that pays her Patriots with her Spoils?
In vain at Court the Bankrupt pleads his cause,
His thankless Country leaves him to her Laws.

The Sense to value Riches, with the Art
T'enjoy them, and the Virtue to impart,
Not meanly, nor ambitiously pursu'd,
Not sunk by sloth, nor rais'd by servitude;
To balance Fortune by a just expence,
Join with Oeconomy, Magnificence;
With Splendour, Charity; with Plenty, Health;
Oh teach us, BATHURST! yet unspoil'd by wealth!
That secret rare, between th' extremes to move
Of mad Good-nature, and of mean Self-love.

To Want or Worth well-weigh'd, be Bounty giv'n,
And ease, or emulate, the care of Heav'n,
Whose measure full o'erflows on human race;
Mend Fortune's fault, and justify her grace.
Wealth in the gross is death, but life diffus'd,
As Poison heals, in just proportion us'd:
In heaps, like Ambergrise, a stink it lies,
But well-dispers'd, is Incense to the Skies.

Who starves by Nobles, or with Nobles eats?
The Wretch that trusts them, and the Rogue that
        cheats.
Is there a Lord, who knows a cheerful noon
Without a Fiddler, Flatt'rer, or Buffoon?
Whose table, Wit, or modest Merit share,
Un-elbow'd by a Gamester, Pimp, or Play'r?
Who copies Your's, or OXFORD's better part,
To ease th' oppress'd, and raise the sinking heart?
Where-e'er he shines, oh Fortune, gild the scene,
And Angels guard him in the golden Mean!
There, English Bounty yet a-while may stand,
And Honour linger ere it leaves the land.

An Epistle from Mr. Pope, to Dr. Arbuthnot

Neque sermonibus Vulgi *dederis te, nec in* Præmiis *humanis spem poseuris rerum tuarum: suis te oportet illecebris* ipsa Virtus *trahat ad verum decus. Quid de te alii loquantur, ipsi videant, sed loquentur tamen.*

TULLY (*De Re Publica*, Lib. VI, cap. XXIII)

ADVERTISEMENT

This Paper is a Sort of Bill of Complaint, begun many years since, and drawn up by snatches, as the several Occasions offer'd. I had no thoughts of publishing it, till it pleas'd some Persons of Rank and Fortune (the Authors of Verses to the Imitator of Horace, *and of an* Epistle to a Doctor of Divinity from a Nobleman at Hampton Court,) *to attack in a very extra-ordinary manner, not only my Writings (of which being publick the Publick judge) but my* Person, Morals, *and* Family, *whereof to those who know me not, a truer Information may be requisite. Being divided between the Necessity to say something of* Myself, *and my own Laziness to undertake so awkward a Task, I thought it the shortest way to put the last hand to this Epistle. If it have any thing pleasing, it will be That by which I am most desirous to please, the* Truth *and the* Sentiment; *and if any thing offensive, it will be only to those I am least sorry to offend, the* Vicious *or the* Ungenerous.

Many will know their own Pictures in it, there being not a Circumstance but what is true; but I have, for the most part spar'd their Names, and they may escape being laugh'd at, if they please.

I would have some of them know, it was owing to the Request of the learned and candid Friend to whom it is inscribed, that I make not as free use of theirs as they have done of mine. However I shall have this Advantage, and Honour, on my side, that whereas by their proceeding, any Abuse may be directed at any man, no Injury can possibly be done by mine, since a Nameless

119

Character can never be found out, but by its Truth *and* Likeness.

Shut, shut the door, good *John!* fatigu'd I said,
Tye up the knocker, say I'm sick, I'm dead,
The Dog-star rages! nay 'tis past a doubt,
All *Bedlam*, or *Parnassus*, is let out:
Fire in each eye, and Papers in each hand,
They rave, recite, and madden round the land.
    What Walls can guard me, or what Shades can hide?
They pierce my Thickets, thro' my Grot they glide,
By land, by water, they renew the charge,
They stop the Chariot, and they board the Barge.
No place is sacred, not the Church is free,
Ev'n *Sunday* shines no *Sabbath-day* to me:
Then from the *Mint* walks forth the Man of Ryme,
Happy! to catch me, just at Dinner-time.
    Is there a Parson, much be-mus'd in Beer,
A maudlin Poetess, a ryming Peer,
A Clerk, foredoom'd his Father's soul to cross,
Who pens a Stanza when he should *engross?*
Is there, who lock'd from Ink and Paper, scrawls
With desp'rate Charcoal round his darken'd walls?
All fly to *Twit'nam*, and in humble strain
Apply to me, to keep them mad or vain.
Arthur, whose giddy Son neglects the Laws,
Imputes to me and my damn'd works the cause:
Poor *Cornus* sees his frantic Wife elope,
And curses Wit, and Poetry, and *Pope*.
    Friend to my Life, (which did not you prolong,
The World had wanted many an idle Song)
What *Drop* or *Nostrum* can this Plague remove?
Or which must end me, a Fool's Wrath or Love?
A dire Dilemma! either way I'm sped,
If Foes, they write, if Friends, they read me dead.

Seiz'd and ty'd down to judge, how wretched I!
Who can't be silent, and who will not lye;
To laugh, were want of Goodness and of Grace,
And to be grave, exceeds all Pow'r of Face.
I sit with sad Civility, I read
With an honest anguish, and an aking head;
And drop at last, but in unwilling ears,
This saving counsel, 'Keep your Piece nine years.'

Nine years! cries he, who high in *Drury-lane*
Lull'd by soft Zephyrs thro' the broken Pane,
Rymes e're he wakes, and prints before *Term* ends,
Oblig'd by hunger and Request of friends:
'The Piece you think is incorrect: why take it,
I'm all submission, what you'd have it, make it.'

Three things another's modest wishes bound,
My Friendship, and a Prologue, and ten Pound.

Pitholeon sends to me: 'You know his Grace,
I want a Patron; ask him for a Place.'
Pitholeon libell'd me—'but here's a Letter
Informs you Sir, 'twas when he knew no better.
Dare you refuse him? *Curl* invites to dine,
He'll write a *Journal*, or he'll turn *Divine*.'

Bless me! a Packet.—' 'Tis a stranger sues,
A Virgin Tragedy, an Orphan Muse.'
If I dislike it, 'Furies, death and rage!'
If I approve, 'Commend it to the Stage.'
There (thank my Stars) my whole Commission ends,
The Play'rs and I are, luckily, no friends.
Fir'd that the House reject him, ' 'Sdeath I'll print it
And shame the Fools—your Int'rest, Sir, with *Lintot*.'
Lintot, dull rogue! will think your price too much.
'Not Sir, if you revise it, and retouch.'
All my demurrs but double his attacks,
At last he whispers 'Do, and we go snacks.'
Glad of a quarrel, strait I clap the door,

Sir, let me see your works and you no more.
  'Tis sung, when *Midas*' Ears began to spring,
(*Midas*, a sacred Person and a King)
His very Minister who spy'd them first,
(Some say his Queen) was forc'd to speak, or burst.
And is not mine, my Friend, a sorer case,
When ev'ry Coxcomb perks them in my face?
'Good friend forbear! you deal in dang'rous things,
I'd never name Queens, Ministers, or Kings;
Keep close to Ears, and those let Asses prick,
Tis nothing'—Nothing? if they bite and kick?
Out with it, *Dunciad!* let the secret pass,
That Secret to each Fool, that he's an Ass:
The truth once told, (and wherefore shou'd we lie?)
The Queen of *Midas* slept, and so may I.
  You think this cruel? take it for a rule,
No creature smarts so little as a Fool.
Let Peals of Laughter, *Codrus!* round thee break,
Thou unconcern'd canst hear the mighty Crack.
Pit, Box and Gall'ry in convulsions hurl'd,
Thou stand'st unshook amidst a bursting World.
Who shames a Scribler? break one cobweb thro',
He spins the slight, self-pleasing thread anew;
Destroy his Fib, or Sophistry; in vain,
The Creature's at his dirty work again;
Thron'd in the Centre of his thin designs;
Proud of a vast Extent of flimzy lines.
Whom have I hurt? has Poet yet, or Peer,
Lost the arch'd eye-brow, or *Parnassian* sneer?
And has not *Colly* still his Lord, and Whore?
His Butchers *Henley*, his Free-masons *Moor?*
Does not one Table *Bavius* still admit?
Still to one Bishop *Philips* seem a Wit?
Still *Sapho*—'Hold! for God-sake—you'll offend:
No Names—be calm—learn Prudence of a Friend:

I too could write, and I am twice as tall,
But Foes like these!'—One Flatt'rer's worse than all;
Of all mad Creatures, if the Learn'd are right,
It is the Slaver kills, and not the Bite.
A Fool quite angry is quite innocent;
Alas! 'tis ten times worse when they *repent*.

One dedicates, in high Heroic prose,
And ridicules beyond a hundred foes;
One from all *Grubstreet* will my fame defend,
And, more abusive, calls himself my friend.
This prints my Letters, that expects a Bribe,
And others roar aloud, 'Subscribe, subscribe.'
There are, who to my Person pay their court,
I cough like *Horace*, and tho' lean, am short,
Ammon's great Son one shoulder had too high,
Such *Ovid*'s nose, and 'Sir! you have an *Eye*—'
Go on, obliging Creatures, make me see
All that disgrac'd my Betters, met in me:
Say for my comfort, languishing in bed,
'Just so immortal *Maro* held his head:'
And when I die, be sure you let me know
Great *Homer* dy'd three thousand years ago.

Why did I write? what sin to me unknown
Dipt me in Ink, my Parents', or my own?
As yet a Child, nor yet a Fool to Fame,
I lisp'd in Numbers, for the Numbers came.
I left no Calling for this idle trade,
No Duty broke, no Father dis-obey'd.
The Muse but serv'd to ease some Friend, not Wife,
To help me thro' this long Disease, my Life,
To second, ARBUTHNOT! thy Art and Care,
And teach, the Being you preserv'd, to bear.

But why then publish? *Granville* the polite,
And knowing *Walsh*, would tell me I could write;
Well-natur'd *Garth* inflam'd with early praise,
And *Congreve* lov'd, and *Swift* endur'd my Lays;
The Courtly *Talbot*, *Somers*, *Sheffield* read,
Ev'n mitred *Rochester* would nod the head,
And *St. John*'s self (great *Dryden*'s friends before)
With open arms receiv'd one Poet more.
Happy my Studies, when by these approv'd!
Happier their Author, when by these belov'd!
From these the world will judge of Men and Books,
Not from the *Burnets*, *Oldmixons*, and *Cooks*.

Soft were my Numbers, who could take offence
While pure Description held the place of Sense?
Like gentle *Fanny*'s was my flow'ry Theme,
A painted Mistress, or a purling Stream.
Yet then did *Gildon* draw his venal quill;
I wish'd the man a dinner, and sate still:
Yet then did *Dennis* rave in furious fret;
I never answer'd, I was not in debt:
If want provok'd, or madness made them print,
I wag'd no war with *Bedlam* or the *Mint*.

Did some more sober Critic come abroad?
If wrong, I smil'd; if right, I kiss'd the rod.
Pains, reading, study, are their just pretence,
And all they want is spirit, taste, and sense.
Comma's and points they set exactly right,
And 'twere a sin to rob them of their Mite.
Yet ne'r one sprig of Laurel grac'd these ribalds,
From slashing *Bentley* down to pidling *Tibalds*.
Each Wight who reads not, and but scans and spells,
Each Word-catcher that lives on syllables,
Ev'n such small Critics some regard may claim,
Preserv'd in *Milton*'s or in *Shakespear*'s name.
Pretty! in Amber to observe the forms

Of hairs, or straws, or dirt, or grubs, or worms;
The things, we know, are neither rich nor rare,
But wonder how the Devil they got there?
    Were others angry? I excus'd them too;
Well might they rage; I gave them but their due.
A man's true merit 'tis not hard to find,
But each man's secret standard in his mind,
That Casting-weight Pride adds to Emptiness,
This, who can gratify? for who can *guess*?
The Bard whom pilf'red Pastorals renown,
Who turns a *Persian* Tale for half a crown,
Just writes to make his barrenness appear,
And strains from hard-bound brains eight lines a-year:
He, who still wanting tho' he lives on theft,
Steals much, spends little, yet has nothing left:
And he, who now to sense, now nonsense leaning,
Means not, but blunders round about a meaning:
And he, whose Fustian's so sublimely bad,
It is not Poetry, but Prose run mad:
All these, my modest Satire bad *translate*,
And own'd, that nine such Poets made a *Tate*.
How did they fume, and stamp, and roar, and chafe?
And swear, not *Addison* himself was safe.
    Peace to all such! but were there One whose fires
True Genius kindles, and fair Fame inspires,
Blest with each Talent and each Art to please,
And born to write, converse, and live with ease:
Shou'd such a man, too fond to rule alone,
Bear, like the *Turk*, no brother near the throne,
View him with scornful, yet with jealous eyes,
And hate for Arts that caus'd himself to rise;
Damn with faint praise, assent with civil leer,
And without sneering, teach the rest to sneer;
Willing to wound, and yet afraid to strike,
Just hint a fault, and hesitate dislike;

Alike reserv'd to blame, or to commend,
A tim'rous foe, and a suspicious friend,
Dreading ev'n fools, by Flatterers besieg'd,
And so obliging that he ne'er oblig'd;
Like *Cato*, give his little Senate laws,
And sit attentive to his own applause;
While Wits and Templers ev'ry sentence raise,
And wonder with a foolish face of praise.
Who but must laugh, if such a man there be?
Who would not weep, if *Atticus* were he!

   What tho' my Name stood rubric on the walls?
Or plaister'd posts, with Claps in capitals?
Or smoaking forth, a hundred Hawkers load,
On Wings of Winds came flying all abroad?
I sought no homage from the Race that write;
I kept, like *Asian* Monarchs, from their sight:
Poems I heeded (now be-rym'd so long)
No more than Thou, great GEORGE! a Birth-day Song.
I ne'r with Wits or Witlings past my days,
To spread about the Itch of Verse and Praise;
Nor like a Puppy daggled thro' the Town,
To fetch and carry Sing-song up and down;
Nor at Rehearsals sweat, and mouth'd, and cry'd,
With Handkerchief and Orange at my side:
But sick of Fops, and Poetry, and Prate,
To *Bufo* left the whole *Castalian* State.

   Proud, as *Apollo* on his forked hill,
Sate full-blown *Bufo*, puff'd by ev'ry quill;
Fed with soft Dedication all day long,
Horace and he went hand in hand in song.
His Library, (where Busts of Poets dead
And a true *Pindar* stood without a head)
Receiv'd of Wits an undistinguished race,
Who first his Judgment ask'd, and then a Place:
Much they extolled his Pictures, much his Seat,

And flatter'd ev'ry day, and some days eat:
Till grown more frugal in his riper days,
He pay'd some Bards with Port, and some with Praise,
To some a dry Rehearsal was assign'd,
And others (harder still) he pay'd in kind.
Dryden alone (what wonder?) came not nigh,
Dryden alone escap'd this judging eye:
But still the Great have kindness in reserve,
He help'd to bury whom he help'd to starve.

    May some choice Patron bless each gray goose quill!
May ev'ry *Bavius* have his *Bufo* still!
So, when a Statesman wants a Day's defence,
Or Envy holds a whole Week's war with Sense,
Or simple Pride for Flatt'ry makes demands;
May Dunce by Dunce be whistled off my hands!
Blest be the *Great!* for those they take away,
And those they left me—For they left me GAY,
Left me to see neglected Genius bloom,
Neglected die! and tell it on his Tomb;
Of all thy blameless Life the sole Return
My Verse, and QUEENSB'RY weeping o'er thy Urn!
Oh let me live my own! and die so too!
('To live and die is all I have to do:')
Maintain a Poet's Dignity and Ease,
And see what friends, and read what books I please.
Above a Patron, tho' I condescend
Sometimes to call a Minister my Friend:
I was not born for Courts or great Affairs,
I pay my Debts, believe, and say my Pray'rs,
Can sleep without a Poem in my head,
Nor know, if *Dennis* be alive or dead.

    Why am I ask'd, what next shall see the light?
Heav'ns! was I born for nothing but to write?
Has Life no Joys for me? or (to be grave)
Have I no Friend to serve, no Soul to Save?

'I found him close with *Swift*'—'Indeed? no doubt'
(Cries prating *Balbus*) 'something will come out.'
'Tis all in vain, deny it as I will.
'No, such a Genius never can lye still,'
And then for mine obligingly mistakes
The first Lampoon Sir *Will.* or *Bubo* makes.
Poor guiltless I! and can I chuse but smile,
When ev'ry Coxcomb knows me by my *Style*?

    Curst be the Verse, how well soe'er it flow,
That tends to make one worthy Man my foe,
Give Virtue scandal, Innocence a fear,
Or from the soft-ey'd Virgin steal a tear!
But he, who hurts a harmless neighbour's peace,
Insults fal'n Worth, or Beauty in distress,
Who loves a Lye, lame slander helps about,
Who writes a Libel, or who copies out:
That Fop whose pride affects a Patron's name,
Yet absent, wounds an Author's honest fame;
Who can your Merit selfishly approve,
And show the Sense of it, without the Love;
Who has the Vanity to call you Friend,
Yet wants the Honour injur'd to defend;
Who tells whate'er you think, whate'er you say,
And, if he lye not, must at least betray:
Who to the *Dean* and *silver Bell* can swear,
And sees at *Cannons* what was never there:
Who reads but with a Lust to mis-apply,
Make Satire a Lampoon, and Fiction, Lye
A Lash like mine no honest man shall dread,
But all such babling blockheads in his stead.

    Let *Sporus* tremble—'What? that Thing of silk,
Sporus, that mere white Curd of Ass's milk?
Satire or Sense alas! can *Sporus* feel?
Who breaks a Butterfly upon a Wheel?'
Yet let me flap this Bug with gilded wings,

This painted Child of Dirt that stinks and stings;
Whose Buzz the Witty and the Fair annoys,
Yet Wit ne'er tastes, and Beauty ne'er enjoys,
So well-bred Spaniels civilly delight
In mumbling of the Game they dare not bite.
Eternal Smiles his Emptiness betray,
As shallow streams run dimpling all the way.
Whether in florid Impotence he speaks,
And, as the Prompter breathes, the Puppet squeaks;
Or at the Ear of *Eve*, familiar Toad,
Half Froth, half Venom, spits himself abroad,
In Puns, or Politicks, or Tales, or Lyes,
Or Spite, or Smut, or Rymes, or Blasphemies.
His Wit all see-saw between *that* and *this*,
Now high, now low, now Master up, now Miss,
And he himself one vile Antithesis.
Amphibious Thing! that acting either Part,
The trifling Head, or the corrupted Heart!
Fop at the Toilet, Flatt'rer at the Board,
Now trips a Lady, and now struts a Lord.
Eve's Tempter thus the Rabbins have exprest,
A Cherub's face, a Reptile all the rest;
Beauty that shocks you, Parts that none will trust,
Wit than can creep, and Pride that licks the dust.

  Not Fortune's Worshipper, nor Fashion's Fool,
Not Lucre's Madman, nor Ambition's Tool,
Not proud, nor servile, be one Poet's praise
That, if he pleas'd, he pleas'd by manly ways;
That Flatt'ry, ev'n to Kings, he held a shame,
And thought a Lye in Verse or Prose the same:
That not in Fancy's Maze he wander'd long,
But stoop'd to Truth, and moraliz'd his song:
That not for Fame, but Virtue's better end,
He stood the furious Foe, the timid Friend,
The damning Critic, half-approving Wit,

The Coxcomb hit, or fearing to be hit;
Laugh'd at the loss of Friends he never had,
The dull, the proud, the wicked, and the mad;
The distant Threats of Vengeance on his head,
The Blow unfelt, the Tear he never shed;
The Tale reviv'd, the Lye so oft o'erthrown;
Th' imputed Trash and Dulness not his own;
The Morals blacken'd when the Writings scape;
The libel'd Person, and the pictur'd Shape;
Abuse on all he lov'd, or lov'd him, spread,
A Friend in Exile, or a Father, dead;
The Whisper that to Greatness still too near,
Perhaps, yet vibrates on his SOVEREIGN's Ear—
Welcome for thee, fair Virtue! all the past:
For thee, fair Virtue! welcome ev'n the *last!*

   'But why insult the Poor, affront the Great?'
A Knave's a Knave, to me, in ev'ry State,
Alike my scorn, if he succeed or fail,
Sporus at Court, or *Japhet* in a Jayl,
A hireling Scribler, or a hireling Peer,
Knight of the Post corrupt, or of the Shire,
If on a Pillory, or near a Throne,
He gain his Prince's Ear, or lose his own.

   Yet soft by Nature, more a Dupe than Wit,
Sapho can tell you how this Man was bit
This dreaded Sat'rist *Dennis* will confess
Foe to his Pride, but Friend to his Distress:
So humble, he has knock'd at *Tibbald*'s door,
Has drunk with *Cibber*, nay has rym'd for *Moor*.
Full ten years slander'd, did he once reply?
Three thousand Suns went down on *Welsted*'s Lye:
To please a *Mistress*, One aspers'd his life;
He lash'd him not, but let her be his *Wife*:
Let *Budgel* charge low *Grubstreet* on his quill,
And write whate'er he pleas'd, except his *Will*;

Let the *Two Curls* of Town and Court, abuse
His Father, Mother, Body, Soul, and Muse.
Yet why? that Father held it for a rule
It was a Sin to call our Neighbour Fool,
That harmless Mother thought no Wife a Whore,—
Hear this! and spare his Family, *James More!*
Unspotted Names! and memorable long,
If there be Force in Virtue, or in Song.

Of gentle Blood (part shed in Honour's Cause,
While yet in *Britain* Honour had Applause)
Each Parent sprung—'What Fortune, pray?'—
    Their own,
And better got than *Bestia's* from the Throne.
Born to no Pride, inheriting no Strife,
Nor marrying Discord in a Noble Wife,
Stranger to Civil and Religious Rage,
The good Man walk'd innoxious thro' his Age.
No Courts he saw, no Suits would ever try,
Nor dar'd an Oath, nor hazarded a Lye:
Un-learn'd, he knew no Schoolman's subtle Art,
No Language, but the Language of the Heart.
By Nature honest, by Experience wise,
Healthy by Temp'rance and by Exercise:
His Life, tho' long, to sickness past unknown,
His Death was instant, and without a groan.
Oh grant me thus to live, and thus to die!
Who sprung from Kings shall know less joy than I.

O Friend! may each Domestick Bliss be thine!
Be no unpleasing Melancholy mine:
Me, let the tender Office long engage
To rock the Cradle of reposing Age,
With lenient Arts extend a Mother's breath,
Make Languor smile, and smooth the Bed of Death,
Explore the Thought, explain the asking Eye,
And keep a while one Parent from the Sky!

On Cares like these if Length of days attend,
May Heav'n, to bless those days, preserve my Friend,
Preserve him social, chearful, and serene,
And just as rich as when he serv'd a QUEEN!
Whether that Blessing be deny'd, or giv'n,
Thus far was right, the rest belongs to Heav'n.

The First Epistle of the Second Book
of Horace Imitated

TO AUGUSTUS

Ne Rubeam, pingui donatus Munere!
HOR. (*Ep. II. i. 267*)

EXTRACTS

(*lines 79–160*)

'Yet surely, surely, these were famous men!
What Boy but hears the sayings of old Ben?
In all debates where Criticks bear a part,
Not one but nods, and talks of Johnson's Art,
Of Shakespear's Nature, and of Cowley's Wit;
How Beaumont's Judgment check'd what Fletcher
    writ;
How Shadwell hasty, Wycherly was slow;
But, for the Passions, Southern sure and Rowe.
These, only these, support the crouded stage,
From eldest Heywood down to Cibber's age.'

All this may be; the People's Voice is odd,
It is, and it is not, the voice of God.
To Gammer Gurton if it give the bays,
And yet deny the Careless Husband praise,

132

Or say our fathers never broke a rule;
Why then I say, the Publick is a fool.
But let them own, that greater faults than we
They had, and greater Virtues, I'll agree.
Spenser himself affects the obsolete,
And Sydney's verse halts ill on Roman feet:
Milton's strong pinion now not Heav'n can bound,
Now serpent-like, in prose he sweeps the ground,
In Quibbles, Angel and Archangel join,
And God the Father turns a School-Divine.
Not that I'd lop the Beauties from his book,
Like slashing Bentley with his desp'rate Hook;
Or damn all Shakespear, like th' affected fool
At Court, who hates what'er he read at School.

But for the Wits of either Charles's days,
The Mob of Gentlemen who wrote with Ease;
Sprat, Carew, Sedley, and a hundred more,
(Like twinkling Stars the Miscellanies o'er)
One Simile, that solitary shines
In the dry Desert of a thousand lines,
Or lengthen'd Thought that gleams thro' many a
       page,
Has sanctify'd whole Poems for an age.

I lose my patience, and I own it too,
When works are censur'd, not as bad, but new;
While if our Elders break all Reason's laws,
These fools demand not Pardon, but Applause.

On Avon's bank, where flow'rs eternal blow,
If I but ask, if any weed can grow?
One Tragic sentence if I dare deride
Which Betterton's grave Action dignify'd,
Or well-mouth'd Booth with emphasis proclaims,
(Tho' but, perhaps, a muster-roll of Names)
How will our Fathers rise up in a rage,
And swear, all shame is lost in George's Age!

You'd think no Fools disgrac'd the former Reign,
Did not some grave Examples yet remain,
Who scorn a Lad should teach his Father skill,
And, having once been wrong, will be so still.
He, who to seem more deep than you or I,
Extols old Bards, or Merlin's Prophecy,
Mistake him not; he envies, not admires,
And to debase the Sons, exalts the Sires.
Had ancient Times conspir'd to dis-allow
What then was new, what had been ancient now?
Or what remain'd, so worthy to be read
By learned Criticks, of the mighty Dead?
  In Days of Ease, when now the weary Sword
Was sheath'd, and *Luxury* with *Charles* restor'd;
In every Taste of foreign Courts improv'd,
'All by the King's Example, liv'd and lov'd.'
Then Peers grew proud in Horsemanship t' excell,
New-market's Glory rose, as Britain's fell;
The Soldier breath'd the Gallantries of France,
And ev'ry flow'ry Courtier writ Romance.
Then Marble soften'd into life grew warm,
And yielding Metal flow'd to human form:
Lely on animated Canvas stole
The sleepy Eye, that spoke the melting soul.
No wonder then, when all was Love and Sport,
The willing Muses were debauch'd at Court;
On each enervate string they taught the Note
To pant, or tremble thro' an Eunuch's throat.
But Britain, changeful as a Child at play,
Now calls in Princes, and now turns away.
Now Whig, now Tory, what we lov'd we hate;
Now all for Pleasure, now for Church and State;
Now for Prerogative, and now for Laws;
Effects unhappy! from a Noble Cause.

We conquer'd France, but felt our captive's
    charms;
Her Arts victorious triumph'd o'er our Arms:
Britain to soft refinements less a foe,
Wit grew polite, and Numbers learn'd to flow.
Waller was smooth; but Dryden taught to join ⎱
The varying verse, the full resounding line,   ⎬
The long majestic march, and energy divine. ⎰
Tho' still some traces of our rustic vein
And splay-foot verse, remain'd, and will remain.
Late, very late, correctness grew our care,
When the tir'd nation breath'd from civil war.
Exact Racine, and Corneille's noble fire
Show'd us that France had something to admire.
Not but the Tragic spirit was our own,
And full in Shakespear, fair in Otway shone:
But Otway fail'd to polish or refine,
And fluent Shakespear scarce effac'd a line.
Ev'n copious Dryden, wanted, or forgot,
The last and greatest Art, the Art to blot.

  Some doubt, if equal pains or equal fire
The humbler Muse of Comedy require?
But in known Images of life I guess
The labour greater, as th' Indulgence less.
Observe how seldom ev'n the best succeed:
Tell me if Congreve's Fools are Fools indeed?
What pert low Dialogue had Farqu'ar writ!
How Van wants grace, who never wanted wit!
The stage how loosely does Astræa tread,
Who fairly puts all Characters to bed:
And idle Cibber, how he breaks the laws,
To make poor Pinky eat with vast applause!
But fill their purse, our Poet's work is done,

Alike to them, by Pathos or by Pun.

    O you! whom Vanity's light bark conveys
On Fame's mad voyage by the wind of Praise;
With what a shifting gale your course you ply;
For ever sunk too low, or born too high!
Who pants for glory finds but short repose,
A breath revives him, or a breath o'erthrows!
Farewel the stage! if just as thrives the Play,
The silly bard grows fat, or falls away.

    There still remains to mortify a Wit,
The many-headed Monster of the Pit:
A sense-less, worth-less, and unhonour'd crowd;
Who to disturb their betters mighty proud,
Clatt'ring their sticks, before ten lines are spoke,
Call for the Farce, the Bear, or the Black-joke.
What dear delight to Britons Farce affords!
Farce once the taste of Mobs, but now of Lords;
(For Taste, eternal wanderer, now flies
From heads to ears, and now from ears to eyes.)
The Play stands still; damn action and discourse,
Back fly the scenes, and enter foot and horse;
Pageants on pageants, in long order drawn,
Peers, Heralds, Bishops, Ermin, Gold, and Lawn;
The Champion too! and, to complete the jest,
Old Edward's Armour beams on Cibber's breast!
With laughter sure Democritus had dy'd,
Had he beheld an Audience gape so wide.
Let Bear or Elephant be e'er so white,
The people, sure, the people are the sight!
Ah luckless Poet! stretch thy lungs and roar,
That Bear or Elephant shall heed thee more
While all its throats the Gallery extends,
And all the Thunder of the Pit ascends!
Loud as the Wolves on Orcas' stormy steep,
Howl to the roarings of the Northern deep.

Such is the shout, the long-applauding note,
At Quin's high plume, or Oldfield's pettitcoat,
Or when from Court a birth-day suit bestow'd
Sinks the lost Actor in the tawdry load.
Booth enters—hark! the Universal Peal!
'But has he spoken?' Not a syllable.
'What shook the stage, and made the people stare?'
Cato's long Wig, flowr'd gown, and lacquer'd chair.

The Second Epistle of the Second Book
of Horace Imitated

Ludentis speciem dabit & torquebitur—
HOR. (*Ep. II. ii. 124.*)

EXTRACT

(lines 153–179)

In vain, bad Rhimers all mankind reject,
They treat themselves with most profound respect;
'Tis to small purpose that you hold your tongue,
Each prais'd within, is happy all day long.
But how severely with themselves proceed
The Men, who write such Verses as we can read?
Their own strict Judges, not a word they spare
That wants or Force, or Light, or Weight, or Care,
Howe'er unwillingly it quits its place,
Nay tho' at Court (perhaps) it may find grace:
Such they'll degrade; and sometimes, in its stead,
In downright Charity revive the dead;
Mark where a bold expressive Phrase appears,
Bright thro' the rubbish of some hundred years;

Command old words that long have slept, to wake,
Words, that wise *Bacon*, or brave *Raleigh* spake;
Or bid the new be *English*, Ages hence,
(For Use will father what's begot by Sense)
Pour the full Tide of Eloquence along,
Serenely pure, and yet divinely strong,
Rich with the Treasures of each foreign Tongue;
Prune the luxuriant, the uncouth refine,
But show no mercy to an empty line;
Then polish all, with so much life and ease,
You think 'tis Nature, and a knack to please:
'But Ease in writing flows from Art, not Chance,
As those move easiest who have learn'd to dance.'

The Seventh Epistle of
the First Book of Horace

IMITATED IN THE MANNER OF DR. SWIFT

'Tis true, my Lord, I gave my word,
I would be with you, June the third;
Chang'd it to August, and (in short)
Have kept it—as you do at Court.
You humour me when I am sick,
Why not when I am splenatick?
In town, what Objects could I meet?
The shops shut up in every street,
And Fun'rals black'ning all the Doors,
And yet more melancholy Whores:
And what a dust in ev'ry place!
And a thin Court that wants your Face,
And Fevers raging up and down,
And P—x and P* both in town!

'The Dog-days are no more the case.'
'Tis true, but Winter comes apace:
Then southward let your Bard retire,
Hold out some months 'twixt Sun and Fire,
And you shall see, the first warm Weather,
Me and the Butterflies together.
    My lord, your Favours well I know;
'Tis with Distinction you bestow;
And not to every one that comes,
Just as a Scotsman does his Plumbs.
'Pray take them, Sir,—Enough's a Feast:
Eat some, and pocket up the rest—'
What rob your Boys? those pretty rogues!—
'No Sir, you'll leave them to the *Hogs*.'
Thus Fools with Compliments besiege ye,
Contriving never to oblige ye.
Scatter your Favours on a Fop,
Ingratitude's the certain crop;
And 'tis but just, I'll tell you wherefore,
You give the things you never care for.
A wise man always is or should
Be mighty ready to do good;
But makes a diff'rence in his thought
Betwixt a Guinea and a Groat.
    Now this I'll say, you'll find in me
A safe Companion, and a free;
But if you'd have me always near—
A word, pray, in your Honour's ear.
I hope it is your Resolution
To give me back my Constitution!
The sprightly Wit, the lively Eye,
Th' engaging Smile, the Gaiety,
That laugh'd down many a Summer's Sun,
And kept you up so oft till one;
And all that voluntary Vein,

As when Belinda rais'd my Strain.

A Weasel once made shift to slink
In at a Corn-loft thro' a Chink;
But having amply stuff'd his skin,
Cou'd not get out as he got in:
Which one belonging to the House
('Twas not a Man, it was a Mouse)
Observing, cry'd, 'You scape not so,
Lean as you came, Sir, you must go.'

Sir, you may spare your Application
I'm no such Beast, nor his Relation;
Nor one that Temperance advance,
Cramm'd to the throat with Ortolans:
Extremely ready to resign
All that may make me none of mine.
South-sea Subscriptions take who please,
Leave me but Liberty and Ease.
'Twas what I said to Craggs and Child,
Who prais'd my Modesty, and smil'd.
Give me, I cry'd (enough for me)
My Bread, and Independency!
So bought an Annual Rent or two.
And liv'd—just as you see I do;
Near fifty, and without a Wife,
I trust that sinking Fund, my Life.
Can I retrench? Yes, mighty well,
Shrink back to my Paternal Cell,
A little House, with Trees a-row,
And like its Master, very low,
There dy'd my Father, no man's Debtor,
And there I'll die, nor worse nor better.

To set this matter full before you,
Our old Friend Swift will tell his Story.
'Harley, the Nation's great Support,'—
But you may read it, I stop short.

The Fourth Satire of Dr. John Donne, Dean of St. Paul's, Versifyed

EXTRACT

(lines 226–253)

Painted for sight, and essenc'd for the smell,
Like Frigates fraught with Spice and Cochine'l,
Sail in the *Ladies*: How each Pyrate eyes
So weak a Vessel, and so rich a Prize!
Top-gallant he, and she in all her Trim,
He boarding her, she striking sail to him.
'*Dear Countess*! you have Charms all Hearts to hit!
And '*sweet Sir Fopling*! you have so much wit!'
Such Wits and Beauties are not prais'd for nought,
For both the Beauty and the Wit are *bought*.
'Twou'd burst ev'n *Heraclitus* with the Spleen,
To see those Anticks, *Fopling* and *Courtin*:
The *Presence* seems, with things so richly odd,
The Mosque of *Mahound*, or some queer *Pa-god*.
See them survey their Limbs by *Durer*'s Rules,
Of all Beau-kind the best proportion'd Fools!
Adjust their Cloaths, and to Confession draw
Those venial sins, an Atom, or a Straw:
But oh! what Terrors must distract the Soul,
Convicted of that mortal Crime, a Hole!
Or should one Pound of Powder less bespread
Those Monkey-Tails that wag behind their Head!
Thus finish'd and corrected to a hair,
They march, to prate their Hour before the Fair,
So first to preach a white-glov'd Chaplain goes,
With Band of Lily, and with Cheek of Rose,
Sweeter than *Sharon*, in immaculate trim,
Neatness itself impertinent in him.

The Dunciad in Four Books

Version of 1742

EXTRACTS

BOOK I

(lines 45–84)

In clouded Majesty here Dulness shone;
Four guardian Virtues, round, support her throne:
Fierce champion Fortitude, that knows no fears
Of hisses, blows, or want, or loss of ears:
Calm Temperance, whose blessings those partake
Who hunger, and who thirst for scribling sake:
Prudence, whose glass presents th' approaching jayl:
Poetic Justice, with her lifted scale,
Where, in nice balance, truth with gold she weighs,
And solid pudding against empty praise.
  Here she beholds the Chaos dark and deep,
Where nameless Somethings in their causes sleep,
'Till genial Jacob, or a warm Third day,
Call forth each mass, a Poem, or a Play:
How hints, like spawn, scarce quick in embryo lie,
How new-born nonsense first is taught to cry,
Maggots half-form'd in rhyme exactly meet,
And learn to crawl upon poetic feet.
Here one poor word an hundred clenches makes,
And ductile dulness new meanders takes;
There motley Images her fancy strike,
Figures ill pair'd, and Similies unlike.
She sees a Mob of Metaphors advance,
Pleas'd with the madness of the mazy dance:
How Tragedy and Comedy embrace;
How Farce and Epic get a jumbled race;
Here gay Description Ægypt glads with show'rs,

Or gives to Zembla fruits, to Barca flow'rs;
Glitt'ring with ice here hoary hills are seen,
There painted vallies of eternal green,
In cold December fragrant chaplets blow,
And heavy harvests nod beneath the snow.

All these, and more, the cloud-compelling Queen
Beholds thro' fogs, that magnify the scene.
She, tinsel'd o'er in robes of varying hues,
With self-applause her wild creation views;
Sees momentary monsters rise and fall,
And with her own fool-colours gilds them all.

BOOK II
(lines 235–282)

Now thousand tongues are heard in one loud din:
The Monkey-mimics rush discordant in;
'Twas chatt'ring, grinning, mouthing, jabb'ring all,
And Noise and Norton, Brangling and Breval,
Dennis and Dissonance, and captious Art,
And Snip-snap short, and Interruption smart,
And Demonstration thin, and Theses thick,
And Major, Minor, and Conclusion quick.
'Hold (cry'd the Queen) a Cat-call each shall win;
Equal your merits! equal is your din!
But that this well-disputed game may end,
Sound forth my Brayers, and the welkin rend.'

As when the long-ear'd milky mothers wait
At some sick miser's triple-bolted gate,
For their defrauded, absent foals they make
A moan so loud, that all the guild awake;
Sore sighs Sir Gilbert, starting at the bray,
From dreams of millions, and three groats to pay.
So swells each wind-pipe; Ass intones to Ass,
Harmonic twang! of leather, horn, and brass;
Such as from lab'ring lungs th' Enthusiast blows,

High Sound, attemp'red to the vocal nose;
Or such as bellow from the deep Divine;
There Webster! peal'd thy voice, and Whitfield! thine.
But far o'er all, sonorous Blackmore's strain;
Walls, steeples, skies, bray back to him again.
In Tot'nam fields, the brethren, with amaze,
Prick all their ears up, and forget to graze;
Long Chanc'ry-lane retentive rolls the sound,
And courts to courts return it round and round;
Thames wafts it thence to Rufus' roaring hall,
And Hungerford re-echoes bawl for bawl.
All hail him victor in both gifts of song,
Who sings so loudly, and who sings so long.

This labour past, by Bridewell all descend,
(As morning pray'r, and flagellation end)
To where Fleet-ditch with disemboguing streams
Rolls the large tribute of dead dogs to Thames,
The King of dykes! than whom no sluice of mud
With deeper sable blots the silver flood.
'Here strip, my children! here at once leap in,
Here prove who best can dash thro' thick and thin,
And who the most in love of dirt excel,
Or dark dexterity of groping well.
Who flings most filth, and wide pollutes around
The stream, be his the Weekly Journals bound,
A pig of lead to him who dives the best;
A peck of coals a-piece shall glad the rest.'

BOOK III
(lines 317–332)

'Now Bavius take the poppy from thy brow,
And place it here! here all ye Heroes bow!
This, this is he, foretold by ancient rhymes:
Th' Augustus born to bring Saturnian times.
Signs following signs lead on the mighty year!

See! the dull stars roll round and re-appear.
See, see, our own true Phœbus wears the bays!
Our Midas sits Lord Chancellor of Plays!
On Poets' Tombs see Benson's titles writ!
Lo! Ambrose Philips is prefer'd for Wit!
See under Ripley rise a new White-hall,
While Jones' and Boyle's united labours fall:
While Wren with sorrow to the grave descends,
Gay dies unpension'd with a hundred friends,
Hibernian Politics, O Swift! thy fate;
And Pope's, ten years to comment and translate.

BOOK IV
(lines 9–30)

Now flam'd the Dog-star's unpropitious ray,
Smote ev'ry Brain, and wither'd ev'ry Bay;
Sick was the Sun, the Owl forsook his bow'r,
The moon-struck Prophet felt the madding hour:
Then rose the Seed of Chaos, and of Night,
To blot out Order, and extinguish Light,
Of dull and venal a new World to mold,
And bring Saturnian days of Lead and Gold.

She mounts the Throne: her head a Cloud conceal'd,
In broad Effulgence all below reveal'd,
('Tis thus aspiring Dulness ever shines)
Soft on her lap her Laureat son reclines.

Beneath her foot-stool, *Science* groans in Chains,
And *Wit* dreads Exile, Penalties and Pains.
There foam'd rebellious *Logic*, gagg'd and bound,
There, stript, fair *Rhet'ric* languish'd on the ground;
His blunted Arms by *Sophistry* are born,
And shameless *Billingsgate* her Robes adorn.
Morality, by her false Guardians drawn,
Chicane in Furs, and *Casuistry* in Lawn,

K   145

Gasps, as they straiten at each end the cord,
And dies, when Dulness gives her Page the word.

When thus th' attendant Orator begun.
'Receive, great Empress! thy accomplish'd Son:
Thine from the birth, and sacred from the rod,
A dauntless infant! never scar'd with God.
The Sire saw, one by one, his Virtues wake:
The Mother begg'd the blessing of a Rake.
Thou gav'st that Ripeness, which so soon began,
And ceas'd so soon, he ne'er was Boy, nor Man.
Thro' School and College, thy kind cloud o'ercast,
Safe and unseen the young Æneas past:
Thence bursting glorious, all at once let down,
Stunn'd with his giddy Larum half the town.
Intrepid then, o'er seas and lands he flew:
Europe he saw, and Europe saw him too.
There all thy gifts and graces we display,
Thou, only thou, directing all our way!
To where the Seine, obsequious as she runs,
Pours at great Bourbon's feet her silken sons;
Or Tyber, now no longer Roman, rolls,
Vain of Italian Arts, Italian Souls:
To happy Convents, bosom'd deep in vines,
Where slumber Abbots, purple as their wines:
To Isles of fragrance, lilly-silver'd vales,
Diffusing langour in the panting gales:
To lands of singing, or of dancing slaves,
Love-whisp'ring woods, and lute-resounding waves.
But chief her shrine where naked Venus keeps,
And Cupids ride the Lyon of the Deeps;
Where, eas'd of Fleets, the Adriatic main
Wafts the smooth Eunuch and enamour'd swain.

Led by my hand, he saunter'd Europe round,
And gather'd ev'ry Vice on Christian ground;
Saw ev'ry Court, heard ev'ry King declare
His royal Sense, of Op'ra's or the Fair;
The Stews and Palace equally explor'd,
Intrigu'd with glory, and with spirit whor'd;
Try'd all *hors-d'oeuvres*, all *liqueurs* defin'd,
Judicious drank, and greatly-daring din'd;
Dropt the dull lumber of the Latin store,
Spoil'd his own language, and acquir'd no more;
All Classic learning lost on Classic ground;
And last turn'd *Air*, the Echo of a Sound!
See now, half-cur'd, and perfectly well-bred,
With nothing but a Solo in his head;
As much Estate, and Principle, and Wit,
As Jansen, Fleetwood, Cibber shall think fit;
Stol'n from a Duel, follow'd by a Nun,
And, if a Borough chuse him, not undone;
See, to my country happy I restore
This glorious Youth, and add one Venus more.
Her too receive (for her my soul adores)
So may the sons of sons of sons of whores,
Prop thine, O Empress! like each neighbour Throne,
And make a long Posterity thy own.'

BOOK IV

(lines 565 to End)

Next bidding all draw near on bended knees,
The Queen confers her *Titles* and *Degrees*.
Her children first of more distinguished sort,
Who study Shakespeare at the Inns of Court,
Impale a Glow-worm, or Vertu profess,
Shine in the dignity of F. R. S.
Some, deep Free-Masons, join the silent race

Worthy to fill Pythagoras's place:
Some Botanists, or Florists at the least,
Or issue Members of an Annual feast.
Nor past the meanest unregarded, one
Rose a Gregorian, one a Gormogon.
The last, not least in honour or applause,
Isis and Cam made Doctors of her Laws.

Then blessing all, 'Go Children of my care!
To Practice now from Theory repair.
All my commands are easy, short and full:
My Sons! be proud, be selfish, and be dull.
Guard my Prerogative, assert my Throne:
This Nod confirms each Privilege your own.
The Cap and Switch be sacred to his Grace;
With Staff and Pumps the Marquis lead the Race;
From Stage to Stage the licens'd Earl may run,
Pair'd with his Fellow-Charioteer the Sun;
The learned Baron Butterflies design,
Or draw to silk Arachne's subtile line;
The Judge to dance his brother Sergeant call;
The Senator at Cricket urge the Ball;
The Bishop stow (Pontific Luxury!)
An hundred Souls of Turkeys in a pye;
The sturdy Squire to Gallic masters stoop,
And drown his Lands and Manors in a Soupe.
Others import yet nobler arts from France,
Teach Kings to fiddle, and make Senates dance.
Perhaps more high some daring son may soar,
Proud to my list to add one Monarch more;
And nobly conscious, Princes are but things
Born for First Ministers, as Slaves for Kings,
Tyrant supreme! shall three Estates command,
And MAKE ONE MIGHTY DUNCIAD OF THE LAND!'

More she had spoke, but yawn'd—All Nature nods:
What Mortal can resist the Yawn of Gods?

Churches and Chapels instantly it reach'd;
(St. James's first, for leaden Gilbert preach'd)
Then catch'd the Schools; the Hall scarce kept awake;
The Convocation gap'd, but could not speak:
Lost was the Nation's Sense, nor could be found,
While the long solemn Unison went round:
Wide, and more wide, it spread o'er all the realm;
Ev'n Palinarus nodded at the Helm:
The Vapour mild o'er each Committee crept;
Unfinish'd Treaties in each Office slept;
And Chiefless Armies doz'd out the Campaign;
And Navies yawn'd for Orders on the Main.
    O Muse! relate (for you can tell alone,
Wits have short Memories, and Dunces none)
Relate, who first, who last resign'd to rest;
Whose Heads she partly, whose completely blest;
What Charms could Faction, what Ambition lull,
The Venal quiet, and intrance the Dull;
'Till drown'd was Sense, and Shame, and Right, and
        Wrong—
O sing, and hush the Nations with thy Song!

*   *   *

    In vain, in vain,—the all-composing Hour
Resistless falls: The Muse obeys the Pow'r.
She comes! she comes! the sable Throne behold
Of *Night* Primæval, and of *Chaos* old!
Before her, *Fancy*'s gilded clouds decay,
And all its varying Rain-bows die away.
Wit shoots in vain its momentary fires,
The meteor drops, and in a flash expires.
As one by one, at dread Medea's strain,
The sick'ning stars fade off th' ethereal plain;
As Argus' eyes by Hermes' wand opprest,
Clos'd one by one to everlasting rest;

Thus at her felt approach, and secret might,
Art after *Art* goes out, and all is Night.
See skulking *Truth* to her old Cavern fled,
Mountains of Casuistry heap'd o'er her head!
Philosophy, that lean'd on Heav'n before,
Shrinks to her second cause, and is no more.
Physic of *Metaphysic* begs defence,
And *Metaphysic* calls for aid on *Sense!*
See *Mystery* to *Mathematics* fly!
In vain! they gaze, turn giddy, rave, and die.
Religion blushing veils her sacred fires,
And unawares *Morality* expires.
Nor *public* Flame, nor *private*, dares to shine;
Nor *human* Spark is left, nor Glimpse *divine!*
Lo! thy dread Empire, CHAOS! is restor'd;
Light dies before thy uncreating word:
Thy hand, great Anarch! lets the curtain fall;
And Universal Darkness buries All.

Imitations of English Poets:
Earl of Dorset

I. ARTIMESIA

Tho' *Artimesia* talks, by Fits,
Of Councils, Classicks, Fathers, Wits;
   Reads *Malbranche*, *Boyle*, and *Locke*:
Yet in some Things methinks she fails,
'Twere well if she would pare her Nails,
   And wear a cleaner Smock.

Haughty and huge as *High-Dutch* Bride,
Such Nastiness and so much Pride
    Are odly join'd by Fate:
On her large Squab you find her spread,
Like a fat Corpse upon a Bed,
    That lies and stinks in State.

She wears no Colours (sign of Grace)
On any Part except her Face;
    All white and black beside:
Dauntless her Look, her Gesture proud,
Her Voice theatrically loud,
    And masculine her Stride.

So have I seen, in black and white
A prating Thing, a Magpy height,
    Majestically stalk;
A stately, worthless Animal,
That plies the Tongue, and wags the Tail,
    All Flutter, Pride, and Talk.

II. PHRYNE

Phryne had Talents for Mankind,
Open she was, and unconfin'd,
    Like some free Port of Trade:
Merchants unloaded here their Freight,
And Agents from each foreign State,
    Here first their Entry made.

Her Learning and good Breeding such,
Whether th' *Italian* or the *Dutch*,
    Spaniard or *French* came to her;
To all obliging she'd appear:
'Twas *Si Signir*, 'twas *Yaw Mynheer*,
    'Twas *S'il vous plaist*, *Monsieur*.

Obscure by Birth, renown'd by Crimes,
Still changing Names, Religions, Climes,
    At length she turns a Bride:
In Di'monds, Pearls, and rich Brocades,
She shines the first of batter'd Jades,
    And flutters in her Pride.

So have I known those Insects fair,
(Which curious *Germans* hold so rare,)
    Still vary Shapes and Dyes;
Still gain new Titles with new Forms;
First Grubs obscene, then wriggling Worms,
    Then painted Butterflies.

On Silence

IN IMITATION OF THE EARL OF ROCHESTER

Silence! Coœval with Eternity;
Thou wert e'er Nature's self began to be,
'Twas one vast Nothing, All, and All slept fast in thee.

Thine was the Sway, e'er Heav'n was form'd or Earth,
E'er fruitful *Thought* conceiv'd Creation's Birth,
Or Midwife *Word* gave Aid, and spoke the Infant forth.

Then various Elements against thee join'd,
In one more various Animal combin'd,
And fram'd the clam'rous Race of busie Human-kind.

The tongue mov'd gently first, and Speech was low,
  'Till wrangling *Science* taught it Noise and Show,
And wicked *Wit* arose, thy most abusive Foe.

But Rebel Wit deserts thee oft in vain;
  Lost in the Maze of Words, he turns again,
And seeks a surer State, and courts thy gentle Reign.

Afflicted *Sense* thou kindly dost set free,
  Oppress'd with Argumental Tyranny,
And routed *Reason* finds a safe Retreat in thee.

With thee in private modest *Dulness* lies,
  And in thy Bosom lurks in *Thought*'s Disguise;
Thou Varnisher of *Fools*, and Cheat of all the *Wise*.

Yey thy Indulgence is by both confest;
  Folly by thee lies sleeping in the Breast,
And 'tis in thee at last that *Wisdom* seeks for Rest.

Silence, the Knave's Repute, the Whore's good Name,
  The only Honour of the wishing Dame;
Thy very want of Tongue makes thee a kind of Fame.

But could'st thou seize some Tongues that now are free,
  How Church and State should be oblig'd to thee!
At Senate, and at Bar, how welcome would'st thou be!

Yet *Speech*, ev'n there, submissively withdraws
  From *Rights of Subjects*, and the *Poor Man's Cause*;
Then pompous *Silence* reigns, and stills the noisie Laws.

Past Services of Friends, good Deeds of Foes,
  What Fav'rites gain, and what the Nation owes,
Fly the forgetful World, and in thy Arms repose.

The Country Wit, Religion of the Town,
  The Courtier's Learning, Policy o' th' Gown,
Are best by thee express'd, and shine in thee alone.

The Parson's Cant, the Lawyer's Sophistry,
  Lord's Quibble, Critick's Jest; all end in thee,
All rest in Peace at last, and sleep eternally.

Epigrams, Etc.

COUPLET ON HIS GROTTO

And life itself can nothing more supply
Than just to plan our projects, and to die.

EPIGRAM. ENGRAVED ON THE COLLAR OF A DOG WHICH I GAVE TO HIS ROYAL HIGHNESS

I am his Highness' Dog at *Kew*;
Pray tell me Sir, whose Dog are you?

ON QUEEN CAROLINE'S DEATH-BED

Here lies wrapt up in forty thousand towels
The only proof that Caroline had bowels.

EPIGRAM. ON CIBBER'S DECLARATION THAT HE WILL HAVE THE LAST WORD WITH MR. POPE

Quoth *Cibber* to *Pope*, tho' in Verse you foreclose,
I'll have the last Word, for by G—d I'll write Prose.
Poor *Colley*, thy Reas'ning is none of the strongest,
For know, the last Word is the Word that lasts longest.

Ah Bounce! ah gentle Beast! why wouldst thou dye,
When thou had'st Meat enough, and Orrery?

Pope's dog, Bounce, had been entrusted to Lord Orrery, under whose care she died.

Index of first lines and extracts

A Bounce! ah gentle Beast! why wouldst thou dye,   *page* 155
And life itself can nothing more supply   154
A perfect Judge will *read* each Work of Wit   47
A Shepherd's Boy (he seeks no better Name)   41

But anxious Cares the pensive Nymph opprest,   71

Close by those Meads for ever crown'd with Flow'rs,   66

Dear, dam'd, distracting Town, farewell!   81

First follow NATURE, and your Judgment frame   44

Happy the man, whose wish and care   83
Here lies wrapt up in forty thousand towels   154
Here lye two poor Lovers, who had the mishap   90
How much, egregious *Moor*, are we   87

I am his Highness' Dog at *Kew*;   154
In clouded Majesty here Dulness shone;   142
In Miniature see *Nature*'s Power appear;   93
In That blest moment from his Oozy Bed   63
In vain, bad Rhimers all mankind reject,   137

Jove call'd before him t'other Day   84

Know then thyself, presume not God to scan;   94

LEARN then what MORALS Criticks ought to show,   53

Next bidding all draw near on bended knees,   147
Nothing so true as what you once let fall,   103
'Now Bavius take the poppy from thy brow,   144
Now flam'd the Dog-star's unpropitious ray,   145
Now thousand tongues are heard in one loud din: 143

Painted for sight, and essenc'd for the smell,   page 141
Phryne had Talents for Mankind,   151

Quoth *Cibber* to *Pope*, tho' in Verse you foreclose,   154

See! from the Brake the whirring Pheasant springs,   62
She said: the pitying Audience melt in Tears,   77
Shut, shut the door, good *John!* fatigu'd I said,   120
Silence! Coæval with Eternity;   152
Soon as *Glumdalclitch* mist her pleasing Care,   90

Think not by rigorous judgment seiz'd,   89
This having heard and seen, some Pow'r unknown   59
Tho' *Artimesia* talks, by Fits,   150
Thus Criticks, of less *Judgment* than *Caprice*,   48
'Tis true, my Lord, I gave my word,   138

We conquer'd France, but felt our captive's charms;   135
What Nature wants, commodious Gold bestows,   112
When Eastern lovers feed the fun'ral fire,   89
When thus th' attendant Orator begun.   146

'Yet surely, surely, these were famous men!   132